"When an exceptional political theorist comes along to provide nuance to fundamental inquiries about innovation, inequality, and inclusion, it's time to pay attention. While books on innovation abound, Theo Papaioannou's new book is not only a pleasure to read, it is a must-read for anyone thinking of technological advance and a just world."

−Smita Srinivas, Founder Director, The Technological Change Lab, India; and winner of the 2015 EAEPE Myrdal Prize

"As a practitioner of inclusive innovation and social change, this is a must read. Theo Papaioannou presents important moral and political arguments for inclusive innovation and a justice-based framework to transform lives and capabilities. It is the only truly democratic approach to development and growth. I will refer to this book for many years to come."

−Harsha Patel, Chief Executive, Doing Social, UK

"This book elaborates the crucial statement that if innovation and social inclusion should be intimately related, it is urgent to move beyond fair distributions of innovative resources and focus instead on the social relations of knowledge production as well as the production of novel products and services (novel for being inclusive in the sense of solving problems that hamper the fulfilment of basic and yet unsatisfied needs). This standpoint allows for an original, coherent and convincing articulation of diverse perspectives, with particular emphasis on justice and development."

−Judith Sutz, Academic Coordinator, University Research Council, University of the Republic, Uruguay

T0383708

Inclusive Innovation for Development

Innovation has the potential to address a number of development challenges such as combating poverty and delivering health services, but all too often technological progress has failed to consider the needs of the poor, and has actually served to increase inequalities, rather than sharing out the benefits of new technologies and economic growth. *Inclusive Innovation for Development* outlines a theory of justice in innovation, arguing that principles of equity, recognition and participation can guide the direction of contemporary innovation systems towards equalising social relations in the production of knowledge and innovation, and meeting the basic needs of the poor.

The book first explores why inclusivity in innovation matters, and how the justice framework can be used to support inclusive innovation. The book then goes on to outline a 'needs-based' approach to innovation and development and explains how its principles can be generated through public action. Finally, it asks how we can effectively evaluate inclusive innovation. Drawing on cases from Africa, Latin America and South Asia, this book theorises innovation and justice in political terms, arguing that inclusive innovation is not just a practical necessity but a moral obligation.

This book's novel approach to innovation for development will be useful for upper-level students and scholars of development studies, politics, and innovation studies, as well as to local, national and international policy-makers and practitioners dealing with international development and inclusive innovation policies and programmes.

Theo Papaioannou is Professor of Politics, Innovation and Development at the Open University, UK. He has researched and published extensively in the areas of political theory and public policy with a focus on innovation and development. His recent books include: (with Butcher, M.) *International Development in a Changing World*, 2013, and *Reading Hayek in the 21st Century: A Critical Inquiry into his Political Theory*, 2012.

Routledge Studies in Development and Society

Dislocation and Resettlement in Development
From Third World to the World of the Third
Anjan Chakrabarti and Anup Kumar Dhar

Community Development in Asia and the Pacific
Manohar S. Pawar

Development Poverty and Politics
Putting Communities in the Driver's Seat
Richard Martin and Ashna Mathema

Protecting Biological Diversity
The Effectiveness of Access and Benefit-sharing Regimes
Carmen Richerzhagen

Social Development
Critical Themes and Perspectives
Edited by Manohar S. Pawar and David R. Cox

India's New Economic Policy
A Critical Analysis
Edited by Waquar Ahmed, Amitabh Kundu and Richard Peet

Towards Sustainable Rural Regions in Europe
Exploring Inter-Relationships Between Rural Policies, Farming,
Environment, Demographics, Regional Economies and Quality of Life
Using System Dynamics
*Edited by John M. Bryden, Sophia Efstratoglou, Tibor Ferenczi, Karlheinz
Knickel, Tom Johnson, Karen Refsgaard and Kenneth J. Thomson*

Inclusive Innovation for Development

Meeting the Demands of Justice
through Public Action

Theo Papaioannou

Routledge
Taylor & Francis Group

LONDON AND NEW YORK

First published 2018
by Routledge
2 Park Square, Milton Park, Abingdon, Oxon OX14 4RN

and by Routledge
52 Vanderbilt Avenue, New York, NY 10017

First issued in paperback 2020

Routledge is an imprint of the Taylor & Francis Group, an informa business

British Library Cataloguing-in-Publication Data
A catalogue record for this book is available from the British Library

Library of Congress Cataloging-in-Publication Data
A catalog record has been requested for this book

ISBN 13: 978-0-367-67046-7 (pbk)
ISBN 13: 978-1-138-30486-4 (hbk)

Typeset in Times New Roman
by Apex CoVantage, LLC

For Barbara and Dimitri Alexander

Contents

Preface

This small book has been motivated by two well-documented facts of the early 21st century. The first refers to increasing interaction between new technologies and socio-economic inequality across the world. The second refers to emerging models of innovation in developing countries which offer alternatives to social exclusion. It is the lack of theorising of both of these facts, together with what I view as an unsatisfactory engagement with alternative perspectives of new knowledge development, that has prompted me to work on a predominantly political argument of inclusive innovation for development. My aim in the following chapters is to outline this argument and to clarify a set of normative principles which can guide innovation towards meeting the demands of justice.

As is often the case with research endeavours, this book has benefited from numerous interactions with scholars of innovation and development studies and politics as well as with good friends. I must begin with my colleagues at the Open University (OU), in particular David Wield, Jo Chataway, Norman Clark, Raphie Kaplinsky, Les Levidow, Giles Mohan, Hazel Johnson, Dinar Kale and Maureen Mackintosh all of whom, one way or another, have contributed key ideas and critical arguments to my thinking on inclusive innovation and development. The same holds for my good friends, social theorists Giota Alevizou of the OU and Alex Koutsogiannis of the University of Crete. I owe to them my reflections on new digital technologies and the role of the political state in innovation and development. In addition, it was a pleasure to learn from Smita Srinivas's brilliant work *Market Menagerie: Health and Development in Late Industrial States* (2012). During her generous visits to the OU Innovation, Knowledge and Development (IKD) research centre, I took the opportunity to discuss with her normative and empirical arguments around planning more inclusive innovation systems for development. I am also indebted to Judith Sutz and the late Calestous Juma for discussions in the area of innovation and justice. Conferences such as the Science Policy Research Unit (SPRU) 50th

Anniversary Conference at the University of Sussex in September 2016 helped me clarify my theoretical perspective of emerging models of innovation and development enormously. My wife, Barbara, and our son, Dimitri Alexander, were both supportive of my writing another book (provided it would be relatively small!). I am grateful to Barbara for bearing with my moments of withdrawal and intellectual absorption both in London, UK and South Pelion, Greece.

This book would not have been possible without the support of the OU, in particular the Department of Development Policy and Practice at the School of Politics, Philosophy, Economics, Development and Geography, which approved several study leaves in order to release me from teaching duties and allow me to concentrate on my writing. Routledge and Sage Publications must also be acknowledged for granting me permission to use selected parts from my earlier articles in the academic journals *Innovation and Development* and *Progress in Development Studies*. These articles include: How Inclusive can Innovation and Development be in the Twenty-first Century? (*Innovation and Development*, Vol. 4, No.2, pp. 187–202); Technological Innovation, Global Justice and Politics of Development (*Progress in Development Studies*, Vol. 11, No. 4, pp. 321–338); Sen and Marx on Incentives and Justice: Implications for Innovation and development (*Progress in Development Studies*, Vol.16, No.4, pp. 1–17). Last but not least, I would like to acknowledge with grateful thanks Harriet Powney for her careful editing and preparation of the manuscript, as well as Pauline Hubner for her skilful indexing.

Introduction

Innovation is about novelty. Whether it be doing something (a product or a process) new to the firm, new to the market or new to the world, or something old in new ways, the concept of innovation describes the restless efforts of human beings to provide novel solutions to problems and to transform their technical and socio-economic environment. In this sense, the concept of innovation is rather broad. It is not only concerned with basic and applied research and development (R&D) but also with everyday practices and social institutions. The latter can be transformative of people's lives and capabilities, promoting freedom and democracy.

Since the 1780s, successive technological revolutions have introduced innovations that have had a tremendous impact on the material living conditions of the world population and on human welfare. These innovations range from industrial textiles, railways and electricity to medicines, food processing, automobiles, information and communication technologies (ICTs) and, more recently, to digital technologies, 3D printing, artificial intelligence (AI), nanotechnology, genomics and biotechnology (Juma, 2016; Papaioannou, 2011; Freeman & Soete, 1997). Yet not all individuals and their societies have tasted the fruits of new technologies or shared the benefits of economic growth. There are still people both in the developing regions (e.g. poor people in sub-Saharan Africa and East Asia)[1] and in the developed world (e.g. unemployed people in Europe and the US) who either lack access to new technological products and processes which are of fundamental importance to their well-being, or whose basic needs and interests have never seriously been taken on board in the social process of the generation of innovative technologies (Foster & Heeks, 2013).

Although innovation and technological progress have radically changed the lives of most people across the world, in general they have tended to exclude the very poor, thereby increasing inequalities, spreading starvation, violence and despair around the world (Soares Cluto & Cassiolato, 2013). When I started this book, global income was concentrated among the top 1% (Lazonick & Mazzucato, 2013). More recently, the International Energy Agency revealed that 1.2 billion people have no access to electricity (IEA, 2016). To make matters worse, the availability of medicines in countries such as Tanzania, Kenya, Ghana and Nigeria remains poor (Koivusalo & Mackintosh, 2009) and about 18,000 children per day die from preventable diseases and malnutrition before reaching their fifth birthday (UNICEF, 2013). In terms of global health, almost 90% of resources are spent in addressing the problems of 10% of the world population (mainly those living in the global north), while people in the global south have been excluded from certain developments in health innovation. African countries in particular, as Juma et al. (2001) remind us, have been isolated from the benefits of the global stock of knowledge and its utilisation in the production of innovative goods and services.

This small book is in line with an increasing number of innovation and development scholars (Onsongo & Schot, 2017; Juma, 2016; Heeks et al., 2015; Papaioannou, 2014; Foster & Heeks, 2013; Juma, 2013; Timmermann, 2013; Srinivas, 2012; Cozzens & Kaplinsky, 2009; Srinivas & Sutz, 2008; Cozzens, 2007; Wetmore, 2007; Woodhouse & Sarewitz, 2007; Sutz & Arocena, 2006; Arocena & Sutz, 2003; Arocena & Sutz, 2000; Cozzens et al., 2005; Cozzens et al., 2002) who insist that while innovation has great potential to address a number of grand challenges (e.g. alleviating disease burden and malnutrition, eliminating poverty, delivering good health, security and sustainability), to do so successfully it must be inclusive of the needs and interests of the poor.

However, it also goes a step further in arguing that inclusive innovation is not only a practical necessity but a moral obligation. This obligation and the requirements that are needed to fulfil it depend ultimately upon which particular theory of justice one subscribes to. If that theory is some version of liberal egalitarianism, libertarianism and/or utilitarianism then the scope of justice in innovation is inevitably restricted to the fair distribution of new products and processes. This, however, is unsatisfactory from the point of view of inclusivity because it leaves out questions of relational equality in innovation. In what follows, I therefore suggest that the normative direction of technological innovation in the 21st century should be more radical, transformative and ambitious than simply achieving fair access to resources.

The moral obligation to include the needs and interests of the very poor in innovation demands that we focus on the social process of knowledge generation and the production of new goods and services. To ensure that this process is inclusive and can act to transform human lives and institutions, I propose three overarching and interrelated principles of justice in innovation: equity, recognition and participation. These principles are founded upon public action and campaigning for the equalising of social relations in the innovation process. As such, they can be defended as non-ideal principles which promote a needs-based approach to inclusive innovation and development in the 21st century. Although this approach is rather critical of the application of ideal and constructivist theories of justice in innovation institutions and structures, it does take such institutions to be crucial for meeting the requirements of justice in knowledge generation.

The book is divided into five chapters. Chapter 1 explains why inclusivity in innovation matters. The argument put forward draws on the recent shift from growth to equity and human rights, a shift that demonstrates innovation is not necessarily at odds with social justice. Rather, new technological products and processes can be conducive to what Anderson (1999: 288–289) proposes as the two distinctively political aims of egalitarianism, i.e. to 'end oppression which by definition is socially imposed . . . [and] create a community in which people stand in relations of equality to others'. But the need for a theory that reconsiders inclusive innovation in terms of a plausible argument about justice remains.

Chapter 2 critically discusses what (if anything) existing theories of justice have to offer in the current debate about inclusive innovation. This is an attempt to identify a plausible approach towards generating legitimate principles of just innovation. The chapter clearly demonstrates the poverty of philosophical constructivism and the lack of socio-political foundations of ideal principles. It therefore proposes moving away from liberal egalitarianism, libertarianism, utilitarianism and even parts of capability theory to concentrate instead on defending a 'smarter' needs-based approach to inclusive innovation and development: an approach that is by definition political and that understands innovation as a process embedded in certain socio-economic and political structures.

Chapter 3 further elaborates this alternative approach to justice, explaining how it can answer the question of inclusive innovation for development. It also examines the impact of innovation systems and development on the poor, arguing that emerging models of inclusive innovation in the global south point towards a non-ideal direction of justice. In fact, inclusive innovation for development can only be achieved through public action and campaigning for the meeting of basic needs.

Chapter 4 shows how public action and campaigning can generate non-ideal principles of justice in innovation and how the nature of such principles is not compatible with theoretical construction as a method of generating normative frameworks of innovation and development. Rather, public action and campaigning constitute the source of our three normative principles of inclusive innovation, i.e. equity, recognition and participation. These principles can be justified on the grounds of social relations which are presupposed in the generation and diffusion of new knowledge for pro-poor

4 *Introduction*

products and processes. The achievement of inclusive innovation for development can only ever be possible through the application of equity, recognition and participation, both in realms of production and in the distribution of novel goods and services.

Chapter 5 argues that these non-ideal principles can guide the development of an evaluative framework of inclusive innovation. This justice-based framework can be focused on processes, outcomes and impacts of technological and non-technological innovation. In so doing, it can facilitate the construction of equitable and participatory innovation systems which are able to satisfy people's basic needs, thereby meeting the fundamental demands of social justice.

The book concludes by maintaining that any theory of inclusive innovation must be founded upon a plausible conception of justice. Such a conception cannot be anything other than political. Equity, recognition and participation are justice-based principles which can be applied not only in the distribution of new technological products and processes, but also in their production. Thus, inclusivity is holistically promoted in this book as a moral and political norm in the realms of both production and distribution, thereby satisfying the demands of justice.

Note

1 The term 'developing region' is used here in a rather broad way to include both low- and middle-income countries.

References

Anderson, E. S. (1999) 'What Is the Point of Equality?', *Ethics*, Vol.109, No.2, pp. 287–337.
Arocena, R. and Sutz, J. (2000) 'Looking at National Systems of Innovation from the South', *Industry and Innovation*, Vol.7, No.1, pp. 55–75.
Arocena, R. and Sutz, J. (2003) 'Inequality and Innovation as Seen from the South', *Technology in Society*, Vol.25, pp. 171–182.
Cozzens, S. E. (2007) 'Distributive Justice in Science and Technology Policy', *Science and Public Policy*, Vol.34, No.2, pp. 85–94.
Cozzens, S. E., Bobb, K. and Bortagaray, I. (2002) 'Evaluating the Distributional Consequences of Science and Technology Policies and Programs', *Research Evaluation*, Vol.11, No.2, pp. 101–107.
Cozzens, S. E., Bobb, K., Deas, K., Gatchair, S., George, A. and Ordóñez, G. (2005) 'Distributional Effects of Science and Technology-Based Economic Development Strategies at State Level in the United States', *Science and Public Policy*, Vol.32, No.1, pp. 29–38.
Cozzens, S. E. and Kaplinsky, R. (2009) 'Innovation, Poverty and Inequality: Cause, Coincidence or Co-Evolution?', in B.-A. Lundvall, K. J. Joseph, C. Chaminade

and J. Vang (eds.), *Handbook of Innovation Systems and Developing Countries: Building Domestic Capabilities in a Global Setting*, Cheltenham and Northampton: Edward Elgar.

Foster, C. and Heeks, R. (2013) 'Conceptualising Inclusive Innovation: Modifying Systems of Innovation Framework to Understand Diffusion of New Technology to Low-Income Consumers', *European Journal of Development Research*, Vol.25, No.3, pp. 333–355.

Freeman, C. and Soete, L. (1997) *The Economics of Industrial Innovation*, 3rd ed., London and New York: Routledge.

Heeks, R., Foster, C. and Nugroho, Y. (2015) *New Models of Inclusive Innovation for Development*, London: Routledge.

International Energy Agency (2016) *World Energy Outlook 2016*, Paris: OECD/IEA.

Juma, C. (2013) 'Technological Innovation and Human Rights: An Evolutionary Approach', *Working Paper*, Harvard Kennedy School.

Juma, C. (2016) *Innovation and Its Enemies: Why People Resist New Technologies*, Oxford: Oxford University Press.

Juma, C., Fang, K., Honca, D., Huete-Pérez, J., Konde, V. and Lee, S. H. (2001) 'Global Governance of Technology: Meeting the Needs of Developing Countries', *International Journal of Technology Management*, Vol.22, Nos.7/8, pp. 629–655.

Koivusalo, M. and Mackintosh, M. (2009) 'Global Public Action in Health and Pharmaceutical Policies: Politics and Policy Priorities', *IKD Working Paper No.45*, pp. 1–47.

Lazonick, W. and Mazzucato, M. (2013) 'The Risk-Reward Nexus in the Innovation-Inequality Relationship: Who Takes the Risks? Who Gets the Rewards?', *Industrial and Corporate Change*, Vol.22, No.4, pp. 1093–1128.

Onsongo, E. and Schot, J. (2017) 'Inclusive Innovation and Rapid Sociotechnical Transitions: the Case of Mobile Money in Kenya'. Available at: www.johanschot.com/wordpress/wp-content/uploads/2017/02/Onsongo.Schot_.Inclusive-Innovation-Working-Paper-6.2.17.pdf [last accessed 24 January 2018].

Papaioannou, T. (2011) 'Technological Innovation, Global Justice and Politics of Development Progress', *Development Studies*, Vol.11, No.4, pp. 321–338.

Papaioannou, T. (2014) 'How Inclusive Can Innovation for Development Be in the 21st Century?', *Journal of Innovation and Development*, Special Issue: New Models of Inclusive Innovation for Development, Vol.4, No.2, pp. 187–202.

Soares Cluto, M. C. and Cassiolato, J. E. (2013) 'Innovation Systems and Inclusive Development: Some Evidence Based on Empirical Work', paper submitted to the international workshop *New Models of Innovation for Development*, Manchester University.

Srinivas, S. (2012) *Market Menagerie: Health and Development in Late Industrial States*, Stanford: Stanford University Press.

Srinivas, S. and Sutz, J. (2008) 'Developing Countries and Innovation: Searching for a New Analytical Approach', *Technology and Society*, Vol.30, pp. 129–140.

Sutz, J. and Arocena, R. (2006) 'Integrating Innovation Policies with Social Policies: A Strategy to Embed Science and Technology into Development Processes [or sic?]', *IDRC Innovation, Policy and Science Programme Area*, Strategic Commissioned Paper.

Timmermann, C. (2013) *Life Sciences, Intellectual Property Regimes and Global Justice*, PhD Thesis, Wageningen: University of Wageningen.

UNICEF (2013) *Levels and Trends in Child Mortality: Report*, New York: The United Nations Fund.

Wetmore, J. M. (2007) 'Introduction to Special Issue on Science, Policy and Social Inequity', *Science and Public Policy*, Vol.34, No.2, pp. 83–84.

Woodhouse, E. and Sarewitz, D. (2007) 'Science Policies for Reducing Social Inequities', *Science and Public Policy*, Vol.34, No.2, pp. 139–150.

1 Why inclusivity in innovation matters

Until very recently, the unequal generation and diffusion of new technological products and processes through the effects of the globalising market was believed to be necessary in order to foster growth and prosperity in the world. Indeed, the 'Washington Consensus' and the 'Structural Adjustment Programmes' of the World Bank (WB) and the International Monetary Fund (IMF) used to actively promote the neo-liberal orthodoxy of laissez fair in technological innovation and international development. However, this political orthodoxy has clearly failed to deliver inclusive growth while prosperity has equally proven to be a myth – especially for countries in sub-Saharan Africa, East Asia and Latin America (Papaioannou, 2014). Indeed, as Cozzens and Kaplinsky (2009) point out, poverty and deprivation continue to constitute 'the long, low tail of the global diffusion of innovation-driven economic growth'. This is not only disturbing from the point of view of international development but also from the point of view of justice, which demands the treatment of all sorts of inequalities (Barry, 2005), including innovation-generated inequalities, in the world.

This first chapter argues that inclusivity in innovation matters for reducing – or even eliminating – unjust inequalities in the production and diffusion of new technological goods and services. In the next sections I demonstrate that innovation is compatible with the idea of justice. The recent shift in the literature from a focus on growth to a focus on equity and human rights provides us with a good foundation for understanding this compatibility at both the theoretical and practical levels. However, the need for a plausible theory remains. Only by producing a plausible theory of justice in innovation can we address the question of inclusivity in terms of the moral and political obligation to equalise social relations in the generation and distribution of new products and services.

1.1 The shift from a focus on growth to equity and human rights

Since the mid-1990s the perceived relationship between innovation-led growth and inclusive development has been increasingly challenged. Indeed, it has become apparent that social progress is not possible without redistribution and market regulation as the growth process alone has not helped lower-income groups to improve their lives by developing capabilities and taking up equal opportunities. According to a well-known OECD (2013: 5) report, 'a majority of the world poor now live in middle-income countries'. During the last 30 years of neo-liberal experimentation with innovation-led growth, the world has become more economically and socially divided than ever, with the gap between rich and poor within countries widening (Milanovic, 2016).

Table 1.1 shows that between 1981 and 2005, when neo-liberalism was at its peak, some regions (e.g. EAP) registered high growth with substantial poverty reductions, while others (e.g. SAS) – despite their substantial GDP growth – registered little poverty reductions. The reason for this was the increasing inequality in the generation and distribution of innovation-led growth. Even in China, the fact that the economy enjoys a high percentage of growth per capita GDP tells us nothing about precisely *how* this innovation-led growth is generated and distributed within the country (Pogge, 2008). While in India, where half of the global poor live, the fact that the economy enjoys high annual growth has no overall impact on poverty reduction (Kaplinsky, 2011). According to Srinivas (2012), although Indian towns and cities have been long-standing centres of innovation and economic dynamism,

Table 1.1 Per capita GDP growth ($1.25 per day) versus poverty reduction by region, 1981–2005

Region	PC GDP growth 1981–1995	PC GDP growth 1996–2005	$1.25 poverty reduction 1981–1995	$1.25 poverty reduction 1996–2005
East Asia & Pacific (EAP)	6.894	6.355	−5.126	−8.481
Eastern Europe & Central Asia (EECA)	−3.434	4.138	6.769	−2.594
Latin America & Caribbean (LAC)	0.140	1.394	−1.083	−3.176
Middle East & North Africa (MENA)	0.713	2.309	−4.347	−1.445
South Asia (SAS)	3.208	4.143	−1.548	−1.710
sub-Saharan Africa (SSA)	−1.009	1.293	0.644	−1.597

Source: Fosu (2011)

they have not been sites of the just redistribution of resources and/or human capabilities. Certainly, innovation relates to inequality in different ways (World Bank, 2016). Three of which OECD (2013) has clearly identified as related to income: first, in terms of the dispersion of wages among full-time workers and wage dispersions among workers; second, in terms of individuals' earnings; and third, in terms of household earnings and the household market income. But the relationship between innovation and inequality goes beyond simply income. As Cozzens and Kaplinsky (2009: 60) point out, 'Innovation and inequality co-evolve with innovation, sometimes reflecting and reinforcing inequalities and sometimes undermining them'. This co-evolutionary relationship demonstrates one thing in particular: however crucial innovation-led growth may be for economic development, the shift from a focus on this alone to one on equity is necessary if inclusivity and justice are to be achieved. Or, to put it another way, we need to move beyond the traditional Schumpeterian settings of innovation and inequality, and towards equalising the social relations within which innovations are produced – rather than simply those of their diffusion.

It might be argued that the adoption of the United Nations (UN) Millennium Development Goals (MDGs), and the subsequent agreement on Sustainable Development Goals (SDGs), confirmed the normative and practical necessity of shifting the focus from growth to equity, redefining the mission of science, technology and innovation (STI) as the reduction of poverty and the elimination of extreme deprivation. In this sense, achieving the MDGs and the now even more important SDGs

> requires approaches that place science and technology at the centre of development policy in a world that is marked by extreme disparities in the creation of scientific and technical knowledge. The majority of the world's scientific knowledge is generated and utilised in industrialised countries.
>
> (Juma et al., 2001: 630)

Indeed, technological innovations such as genomics and biotechnology can have substantial impact on reducing inequality and improving human health.

In fact, as the UN Millennium Project (2005) had suggested, all eight MDGs could have been met if science, technology and innovation had been made available to developing countries. The same holds true for all 17 of the newly approved SDGs, which emphasise both inclusivity and sustainability in these countries (ICSU, ISSC, 2015). Developing countries have urgent health, agricultural, communication and environmental needs. Addressing these presupposes not only the development of capabilities in developing countries but also the reorientation of innovation towards more inclusive, socially and environmentally just patterns of economic development (UNC-TAD, 2017). More inclusive science and innovation, by definition, implies securing the rights of the poor. Article 27 (1) of the Universal Declaration of Human Rights (UDHR) states: 'Everyone has the right freely to participate in the cultural life of the community, to enjoy the arts and to share in scientific advancement and its benefits'. It thereby places a particular obligation on the advanced developed nations not only to diffuse innovation equally within developing nations, but also to facilitate the creation of their domestic innovative capabilities and capacities. As Juma et al. (2001: 632) argue:

> In contrast to advanced developed nations, developing countries lack many of the ingredients needed for innovation. Opportunities are rare, prompting the analogy of an island of innovation opportunities that must be discovered in a large sea at risk. Most developing countries have only limited indigenous capacity for innovation.

This argument does not imply that developing countries should rely on continuous transfers of technology from developed nations. According to Juma (2013: 6):

> The rights-based approach inspired a naïve view starting in the early 1960s that developing countries could "leap across generations" and industrialise through transfer of technology from industrialised countries. . . . Clauses of "access to and transfer of technology" became major issues of contention between developed and developing countries in various international fora.

This is because a high proportion of the resources which go into innovation remain in the ownership of advanced developed nations.

The granting of exclusive rights to innovators, i.e. intellectual property rights (IPRs) such as patents and copyrights, reinforce the dominance of global innovation hierarchies. 'Many vital medicines and innovations in agriculture are subject to those rights and sold at higher than production prices to allow innovators to recoup research and technology costs' (Timmermann, 2013: 19). Access to these innovations and/or technology transfer is therefore hindered by IPR institutions, resulting in the violation of basic human rights to health and food. This is why the shift from a focus on growth to one on equity and human rights requires a rethinking of the role of IPRs in inclusive innovation and development. IPRs became a global institutional regime through the so-called Trade-Related Aspects of

Intellectual Property Rights (TRIPS) Agreement in 1994, which imposed high standards of IP protection on all World Trade Organisation (WTO) member states. In fact, as Timmermann (2013: 79) stresses, 'Only after the establishment of such an international system of protection of intellectual property rights could concerns about human rights and justice vis-à-vis patents and other forms of intellectual property be sufficiently elaborated'.

However, replacing IPRs on a global scale with a new institutional arrangement and equalising access to innovation and/or the transfer of new technologies does not automatically lead to inclusivity and to meeting the demands of justice. As Juma (2013: 8) reminds us, we should not ignore:

> the fact that technology is usually acquired, not necessarily transferred as right. Technology transfers are limited by factors such as the lack of absorptive capacity in the importing countries. Other facts such as the lack of spare parts supply, differences in ecological conditions and absence of supportive legal environments make it difficult for transplanted technologies to take root.

In the 1970s and early 1980s, the so-called Sussex Manifesto (SM) (Singer et al., 1970) and the Appropriate Technology Movement (ATM) (Schumacher, 1973) made the effort to take on board such contextual factors for the first time. On the one hand, the SM argued that the focus of research and development (R&D) agendas ought to be on the needs of low-income countries. On the other, the ATM promoted the development of new intermediate technologies (ITs) in order to address these needs and improve poor infrastructures in low-income countries. In so doing, both the SM and the ATM attempted to divert technologies towards meeting the development needs of marginalised groups and countries. Such technologies were:

> low in capital cost; reliant on local materials; job-creating, employing local skills and labour; small enough in scale to be affordable for small groups; understood, controlled and maintained by local people wherever possible, without requiring high level of western-style education; involving some forms of collective use and collaboration; avoiding patents and property rights and so on.
>
> (Smith et al., 2017)

The key elements of SM and ATM were social justice and involvement of local communities. Although it is true that both the SM and the ATM offered the prospect of more inclusive and environmentally friendly growth, it is also true that they faced several problems. According to Kaplinsky (2011) the first of these was that most ITs were 'economically inefficient' in the sense that input of capital and labour exceeded the output products. The second was the contextual nature of 'appropriateness' and the disappointment of IT expectations. Finally, the social context of innovation in the developing world was different from that of developed countries, meaning that ITs could not easily scale up.

Despite the failure to fulfil their promise of more equitable growth (ibid.), the SM and the ATM have influenced public actions and campaigns for innovation in many countries. For example, the People's Science Movements (PSMs) in India endorsed the principles of ATM. According to Smith et al. (2017: 86):

> When the PSMs began their efforts in the mid-1980s for the creation of alternative technologies and forms of organisation, two terms were actively under discussion in the discourse on science, technology and society namely, "appropriate technology" and "alternative technology". The early framings of Fritz Schumacher (1973) came to mind, although Gandhi was clearly pioneer and ideological inspiration in India.

This influence confirms the point that inclusive innovation is 'not simply a matter of acquiring and installing machinery, but it entails a transformation of society and its value systems' (Juma, 2013: 9). This transformation ought to take place along the lines of equity in social relations and human rights. In an age of technological abundance, questions of access should be complemented with questions of innovative capabilities building in developing countries.

1.2 Innovation versus justice or justice versus innovation?

Innovation is the main source of dynamism and competitiveness within modern capitalism. Economists who devoted their work to the analysis of capitalist modes of production and social relations recognised this fact quite early. Marx, for instance, directly links technological innovation to the bourgeoisie, arguing that 'they cannot exist without revolutionising the instruments of production and thereby the relations of production and with them the whole of relations of society' (Marx, 2000: 248). In his critique of political economy, innovation is considered to be essential for the continuous development of productive forces and the global expansion of capitalism. Similarly, Schumpeter regards innovation as a key element of capitalist production. For him, innovation is about new combinations of means of production. Schumpeter directly links the innovation process to entrepreneurship. For this reason, he defines the carrying out of new combinations as 'enterprise', and the individuals whose function it is to carry them out as 'entrepreneurs' (Schumpeter, 1983: 74).

However, whether innovation is seen as a matter of entrepreneurship (i.e. a general human activity) or as a bourgeoisie activity (i.e. the activity of a specific social class), Marx and Schumpeter agree in seeing it as the main determinant of economic growth within modern capitalism. For both thinkers 'the growth of productivity and the associated increase in per capita incomes depends upon a continuing process of technological change, involving the introduction of new and improved products and novel ways of organising production, distribution and marketing' (Freeman, 1987: 1).

The recognition of the relationship between innovation, economic dynamism and high rates of productivity growth constitutes the very foundation of today's innovation theory. A number of thinkers, including Freeman and Soete (1997), Edquist (1997), Lundvall (1992), and Nelson and Winter (1977), have argued for the institutional development of national and international innovation systems as a means of strengthening this relationship. Their argument has been influential among development policymakers and practitioners who conceive of technological innovation as the main source of the economic transformation of developing countries.

As was shown earlier, the recent experience of some Asian countries such as China reveals that an increase in scientific and technological capabilities and high rates of economic growth have led to a reduction in the number of people living in absolute poverty. However, as Hanlon et al. (2010: 8) emphasise, 'when you remove China's phenomenal poverty reduction from the 1990–2010 global figures, it becomes clear that life has improved relatively little in the rest of the world'. The reason for this is, as Brock (2009: 222) argues,

> Depending on the distribution of the gains derived from growth, growth can have varying effects. Growth can be measured in terms of GDP per capita. But, since this figure is simply an average for the country, even if the figure increases, we learn nothing about how gains are distributed, and hence nothing about its effects on the poor. Poverty could increase, even with an increase in GDP per capita figure, if gains to the better off outweigh harms to the worst off.

This confirms that it is the *just* generation and distribution of growth that matters in terms of poverty reduction.

Certainly, different – and often competing – accounts of social justice exist. As Buchanan et al. (2011: 308) explain:

> Theorising about justice is notoriously afflicted . . . with both disagreement and uncertainty. There is disagreement between consequentialists and deontologists, between proponents of 'positive' rights and

libertarians, between egalitarians, prioritarians, and sufficientarians, and among egalitarians as to what the 'currency' of egalitarian justice is (well-being, opportunity for well-being, resources or capabilities). In addition there is uncertainty as to how to move from a given theory's abstract, highest-level principles to lower-level principles with clearer implications for policies and institutions.

Although disagreement and uncertainty constitute problems for any theory of social justice, they do not explain why principles of equal distribution of science and technology and innovation have never been a serious concern for innovation theory. Therefore, the question that remains open is: why has innovation theory so far refused to engage with questions of social justice? It might be argued that there are two different but interrelated reasons for this. The first is concerned with the very contradictions of capitalism as an economic and social system of relations. As early as 1848, Marx recognised that the history of modern industry is in fact 'the history of the revolt of modern productive forces against modern conditions of production, against the property relations that are the conditions for the existence of the bourgeoisie and of its rule' (Marx, 2000: 250). Indeed, Marx revealed that technological innovation is at the heart of this contradiction of capitalism. Why is this so? Because technological innovation is presupposed of the development of modern productive forces, forces which in turn have the potential to promote justice.

Buchanan et al. (2011: 308) offer six examples of contemporary technological innovations which have the potential to promote justice by reducing the unjust advantages that some people enjoy, or by empowering people so that they can effectively exercise their individual rights:

1   Some cognitive enhancement drugs are most efficacious for the less bright; to the extent that existing social arrangements unfairly disadvantage those with lower intelligence or lower intelligence results in part from socio-economic injustices, making such drugs available to the latter could be justice promoting. . . .
2   Cheap calculators help 'level the playing field' for those who are mathematically challenged. . . .
3   Medical innovations can remove disabilities that interfere with opportunities individuals ought to have as a matter of justice or that prevent them from exercising their rights.
4   Cell phones allow cheap, rapid co-ordination of economic and political activities; this can help people lift themselves out of poverty. . . .
5   Internet access to medical information reduces knowledge asymmetries between physicians and patients and this in turn can reduce the risk that patients' rights will be violated.

6   Cell phone cameras provide checks on police behaviour, thus helping to reduce violations of civil and political rights.

However, it might be argued that promoting justice through technological innovation threatens the very existence of the private property relations which provide profit incentives for the effective generation of technological innovation. As Dosi et al. (2006: 1110) recognise, 'profit-motivated innovators are fundamental drivers of the "unbound Prometheus" of modern capitalism'. Indeed, this was appreciated by both Marx and Schumpeter. To put it another way, although technological innovation is presupposed of justice, in globalised capitalist societies effective application of principles of equity reduces the profit incentives for technological innovation. It might even be argued that modern innovation theory is rather guilty of ignoring this contradiction. Although there have been critical approaches to technological change, including the SM and the ATM, their proponents (Singer et al., 1970; Schumacher, 1973), while insisting on the role of individuals, firms and institutions in science and technology (S&T) and the development of specific appropriate innovations for developing countries, leave out the questions of whether and how STI can be generated and diffused according to minimum requirements of justice.

It is only very recently that innovation theorists such as, for instance, Onsongo and Schot (2017), Schot and Steinmueller (2016), Heeks et al. (2015), Papaioannou (2014), Cozzens and Sutz (2014), Chataway et al. (2014), Kaplinsky (2011), Cozzens (2007), Eubanks (2007), Woodhouse and Sarewitz (2007), and Arocena and Sutz (2003) have begun to address these questions by examining the application of libertarian, utilitarian, contractarian and communitarian principles of justice in science, technology and innovation. Nevertheless, their view that average inequalities in STI can be eliminated in the long term seems over-optimistic. Equity is not in fact a realistic goal for science and technology unless the incentives for generation and diffusion of innovation change according to the requirements of justice. This is made clear in Table 1.2, which illustrates the level of unequal diffusion of innovation (measured by royalty and license fee payments and receipts) between developed and developing countries before the 2008 global financial crash. Clearly, developing countries pay substantially more in royalty and license fees than they receive. By contrast, developed countries receive substantially more in royalty and license fees than they pay.

This unequal generation and diffusion of innovation based on profit incentives widens the socio-economic gap between and within globalised capitalist societies (Rogers, 1995).

Now, to come to the second reason why innovation theory has so far refused to address questions of justice. This is related to the false assumption

Table 1.2 Royalty and license fee payments and receipts

Countries	Royalty and license fee payments (BoP, current US $) 2007	Royalty and license fee receipts (BoP, current US $) 2007
United States	24,656,000,000	83,824,000,000
Japan	16,677,792,511	23,228,586,013
United Kingdom	10,121,380,039	15,107,533,176
China	8,192,067,402	342,634,075
Brazil	2,259,433,000	319,410,000
India	1,159,824,391	163,126,497
South Africa	1,596,250,885	52,913,602
Mozambique	2,361,671	45,199
Uganda	4,792,886	512,486

Source: World Bank (2010)

that innovation-driven economic growth can be justly diffused through the spontaneous process of the global market. This assumption has led to the problematic conclusion that much of the improvement in human development areas – such as public health, nutrition and agriculture – is due to innovation-driven economic performance and, therefore, that specific justice requirements for equal generation and diffusion of new innovative technologies are not important. Yet it is these requirements which, whether liberal or not, influence human development (Hettne, 2009). This is a development which 'is about more than the rise or fall of national incomes. It is about creating an environment in which people can develop their full potential and lead productive, creative lives in accord with their needs and interests' (UNDP, 2001: 9). This implies that innovation-driven economic performance alone will be unable to address the human development challenges we face in the new millennium, including the morally unacceptable levels of poverty and deprivation in many people's lives.

If it is true that innovation theory has so far refused to engage with questions of justice, it is also true that the theory of justice has so far ignored the prominence of new technologies in the fight against poverty and inequality. With the exception of Hollis and Pogge (2008) and, more recently, Buchanan et al. (2011), the theory of justice has discussed obligations to the poor and questions of distribution without considering the role of innovation in poverty reduction and equal development. Allow me, for instance, to examine the cosmopolitan argument of justice. Contemporary theorists such as Beitz (2008), Nussbaum (2008), Singer (2008), Sen (2009), Caney (2005), O'Neill (2002) and Barry (1998) affirm three principles: individuality, equality and universality. Based on these principles, cosmopolitans try to address three questions: who should be targeted by a global theory of justice? What should be justly distributed? How should goods be distributed? (Papaioannou et al., 2009). In addressing the first question, cosmopolitans agree that it is individuals who should be targeted by a global theory of justice. This answer enables the argument that global distribution applies outside nation states to every individual human being who is the ultimate unit of moral concern. Indeed, according to Caney (2005: 105), 'the most contemporary cosmopolitans affirm that the duties are owed to individuals (and not to states)'.

Cosmopolitan individualism is consistent with human rights requirements. As these requirements concern every individual human being, cosmopolitans consider the international human rights doctrine to be essential in the debate on justice. According to Beitz (2008: 156): 'Human rights are standards intended to play a regulative role for a range of actors in the political circumstances of the contemporary world'. Although cosmopolitans provide important clarifications to the international doctrine of human rights, they do not specify what type of just distribution might possibly meet the human rights requirements. Thus, in addressing the second question – *what* should be justly distributed – cosmopolitans provide different and competing accounts. One school of thought (Beitz, 1999) endorses Rawlsian egalitarianism, arguing that what should be justly distributed are resources. Another (Singer, 2008) reconstructs Bentham's classical utilitarian arguments, insisting that global principles of just distribution should be concerned with welfare and utility. While a third (Sen, 2009; Nussbaum, 2000) maintains that global distributive justice should be concerned with each individual's capabilities to function.

It might be argued that, despite their different and competing accounts, the three schools of cosmopolitan thought implicitly agree on one thing: innovation as such is not highly significant from the point of view of justice. This – problematic, I would argue – agreement becomes clear when one examines the writings of contemporary justice theorists such as Beitz (2008) and Caney (2005) and almost nothing is found about the role of innovation in social justice. There are, of course, several reasons why the theory of justice, generally speaking, has so far refused to engage with questions of technological innovation. Two of these seem to be the most important. The first is concerned with the ideal and constructivist nature of the political concept of justice. Political theorists often fail to question the extent to which their analysis of justice should be governed by judgements about feasibility. Some theorists (e.g. Cohen, 2003) even insist that principles of justice are logically independent of questions about feasibility. In other words, they maintain a clear distinction between the 'ought' of principles of justice and the 'is' of feasibility in contingent historical contexts. This means they not only ignore Marx's and Engels's (1999) critique of abstract, ahistorical and groundless ideal principles, but they also dismiss what Arrow (1997: 759) pointed out in defence of non-ideal principles: 'even if the principles are to be taken as fully valid, their application to a particular situation will usually be complex'. Complexity and historical contingency create limits to the application of principles of justice. Thus, Mason (2004: 253) argues:

> Those who . . . embark upon the conceptual analysis of ideals [such as justice] without considering how these ideals might be realised in the social, political and economic context we confront, are involved in an activity that is inherently limited. Their analyses will possess only marginal political relevance, for they will have no definite practical implications in the absence of an understanding of the causal forces that bear upon implementation.

Indeed, it might be suggested that one of the causal forces that bear upon implementation of principles of justice is innovation. Theories which envisage having high political relevance should acknowledge the importance of innovation in social justice as, on the one hand, the introduction of new technological products and processes has the potential to both ameliorate and to worsen existing social injustices (Buchanan et al., 2011: 310), while, on the other, innovation as such raises new claims of justice. For example, the discovery of a new anti-malarial drug or the development of an innovative vaccine against childhood diseases immediately raises a new claim of their just diffusion to global society – in particular to those who need them most such as low-income populations in developing countries. The same applies to the development of driverless-car technologies and to AI, which raise a new claim for their just diffusion to those who need them most, such as disabled people. Whatever is available to distribute justly thus changes as our productive forces develop through innovation. Or, to put it another way, claims for the just distribution of resources and/or capabilities co-evolve with technical change and innovation. In this sense, the restless moral and political struggle for social justice and equality cannot be divorced from innovation and the system of social relations in which innovative activity takes place.

The second reason why the theory of justice has so far refused to address questions of innovation is based on another false assumption: justice can only be achieved through a deliberate process of global politics. This has led to the problematic conclusion that what is important for the implementation of principles of justice in areas such as global health is not technological innovation but a global political state or a unified sovereign power. For instance, Nagel (2005: 121) argues that 'requirements of justice themselves do not apply to the world as a whole, unless and until, as a result of historical developments . . . the world comes to be governed by a unified sovereign power'. Although Nagel correctly emphasises the importance of politics and the state for the implementation of principles of global justice, he seems to overlook the crucial role of non-state political actors, including non-government organisations (NGOs), global partnerships, global social movements, public actions and campaigns. Indeed, it might be suggested that rather than being limited to the just diffusion of innovation in a global context, their role goes to the very essence of innovation: the generation of new technological products and services which promote global justice. Take, for example, the case of transnational advocacy networks and activism, who not only focus on access to medicines for diseases and issues such as HIV/AIDS, tuberculosis and malaria, but also on pharmaceutical policies for the establishment of essential drugs. International NGOs such as Health Action International (HAI), the Consumer Project on Technology (CPTECH) and Médecins San Frontières (MSF) campaign for specific innovation policies directly relevant to global justice such as the compulsory licensing of patents and exceptions to patent rights for medical research (Koivusalo & Mackintosh, 2009).

However, non-state political actors often do not seem to possess a clear idea of how health innovation should be diffused. Should, for example, it be diffused equally to all, or according to merit or basic human needs? The fact that non-state political actors provide different answers to these questions reflects a disagreement at the normative level of global justice theory. Cosmopolitans, for instance, fail to provide a unified answer to the question of how goods such as innovation should be diffused. More importantly, given the relationship between distribution and production, the cosmopolitan school of thought fails to offer a holistic theory of global justice in innovation. Such a theory should be not so much about the generation and diffusion of new products and services as about the social relations which drive these processes within modern capitalism.

1.3 Why we need a theory

But why attempt to outline a theory of justice in innovation? This is a legitimate question given that, as Barry (2005: 3) observes, 'In the poorest countries, people do not need a theory to tell them that there is something wrong with a world in which the children are dying from malnutrition or diseases that could be prevented'. Indeed, fundamental innovations and inexpensive public health measures could be enough to meet the basic needs of the poor. But not everyone believes that there is a moral and political obligation to include the health needs and interests of the poor in innovation. For neo-liberals, for instance, innovation and development are (and ought to be) market-based processes which create wealth for winners and poverty for losers. Following the theories of Friedrich von Hayek and Ludwig von Mises, neo-liberals insist that these global processes cannot (and should not) be evaluated in terms of universal principles of justice (Papaioannou, 2012; Nederveen Pieterse, 2010).

At this point let me again borrow from Barry (2005: 4) in raising the following question: 'Is it that inequality is wrong or only poverty is bad?' In the area of innovation this question has only just begun to be debated. Specifically, scholars such as Foster and Heeks (2013), Cozzens and Sutz (2012), Srinivas (2012), Cozzens (2007), Eubanks (2007), Woodhouse and Sarewitz (2007), and Arocena and Sutz (2003) provide both empirical and theoretical insights into how innovation can become both more inclusive of the poor and more equitable. However, they disagree about the extent to which such inclusivity can counter-incentivise R&D and entrepreneurial initiatives, especially in developing countries. They also disagree about what obligations, if any, advanced developed countries have towards poorer ones as regards knowledge and technology transfer. It is for this reason that, in a similar way to Barry (2005), I insist that to answer such questions we need a theory – in this case one of global justice in innovation.

Certainly, not all theories of justice (let alone global justice) can provide normative direction to innovation and development. I agree with Barry (2005: 4) that 'we need the right theory . . . if we are to get the right answers. Having the wrong theory may bring about worse results, if it is acted on, than a simple feeling of goodwill towards the human race'. In order to produce the right theory of justice in innovation, in Chapter 2 I shall interrogate different approaches to justice and inclusivity. For the time being, however, allow me briefly to discuss the nature of these concepts.

Most political theorists seem to accept the account of ' "justice as impartiality", where justice requires taking everyone's situation and interests into account in determining what is to count as a just outcome' (Wolff, 2006: 8), while also seeming to:

> converge on the belief that what might be called extreme deprivation is presumptively unjust, at least when it is undeserved. People suffer extreme deprivation when they lack adequate food, shelter, safe drinking water, are afflicted with serious preventable diseases, and when their physical security is seriously compromised by the threat of violence, as in the case of civilians in war zones.
> (Buchanan et al., 2011: 310)

Most theories of justice, meanwhile, from those of Adam Smith (1976) to those of John Rawls (1972) and neo-Rawlsian cosmopolitans such as Charles Beitz (2008, 1999), Thomas Pogge (2002), and Joshua Cohen and Charles

Sabel (2006), would require everyone involved or affected to ask the question: what provisions for the extremely deprived would you want in your society if you did not know whether or not you were to be extremely deprived (Wolff, 2006)? As I will show in the next chapter, these theories overwhelmingly focus on distribution and use conceptual constructions or theoretical devices such as those of the 'impartial spectator' and/or the 'veil of ignorance' to justify 'impartial' principles of justice that individuals would chose in a hypothetical situation in which they are denied knowledge of their own material interests and abilities. Although, by preventing people from choosing principles that serve their individual interests, this might indeed produce fairer principles of justice in innovation and development, it remains an ideal situation inapplicable in the real world of unjust social relations. Empirical problems of innovation-led poverty and inequality cannot be resolved through the application of ideal principles of justice which predominantly focus on distribution. For example, the increasing income and power of the top executives of large companies who fail to take on board – or satisfy – the needs of the poor through markets (Piketty, 2014) cannot be reversed unless public action in this context of non-ideal social relations generates and applies bottom-up principles of equity, recognition and participation.

As far as the field of innovation is concerned, it might be suggested that a suitable theory of justice in innovation should be guided by non-ideal principles which go beyond distribution. This presupposes two things: first, the systematic interrogation of existing egalitarian, libertarian, utilitarian and capability arguments about distributive justice; second, the working out of an alternative theory that can be defended as a relational theory of justice in innovation. The latter, however, cannot be evaluated solely on the grounds of non-ideal principles, but also on whether the application of these principles is likely to resolve what we have called elsewhere (Papaioannou, 2014) the 'innovation-justice trade off', i.e. the trade-off between reducing unjust inequality and increasing incentives for innovation. As Arocena and Sutz (2003: 178) so correctly put it:

> The big question is which types of progress towards . . . less inequality are self-sustaining in the sense that they in turn foster growth and innovation. When this reinforcement occurs, we may speak of proactive or creative equality, i.e. equality that creates more equality by activating innovation capabilities. This refers to processes that, by diminishing inequality in some particular way, expand the social capabilities for social, technological and institutional innovation.

Proactive or creative equality can be thought of as a key non-ideal principle of inclusive innovation. But before I go any further in my analysis

I should clarify the concept of inclusivity which, traditionally, has been defined as the opposite of social exclusion. However, although social exclusion has received tremendous attention since its introduction in the 1970s (Figueiredo & de Haan, 1998; de Haan, 1997; Gore & Figueiredo, 1997; Jordan, 1996; Rodgers et al., 1995; Silver, 1995), inclusivity has been less popular with social scientists and political philosophers. One reason for this may be that the concept of inclusivity is directly related to social equity, equality of opportunity and democratic participation. Thus, it presupposes a multi-dimensional theory of justice that incorporates all these principles. Such a theory is difficult to develop, given the preoccupation of political theory with the fair distribution of income and wealth. Inclusivity describes the processes of equalisation of social relations which prevent people from becoming marginalised and deprived.

Although, as Hickey and du Toit (2007) point out, the concept of inclusivity is not coterminous with poverty reduction, many poor people, especially in the developing world, are not included in (or are excluded from) the benefits offered by globalisation. As Sen (2000: 2) explains:

> Globalisation is both a threat (especially to traditional ways of earning and living) and an enormous opportunity (especially providing new ways of bringing prosperity and affluence). The ability of people to use positive prospects depends on their not being excluded from effective opportunities that globalisation offers (such as new patterns of exchange, new goods to produce, new skills to develop, new techniques of production to use, and so on).

Evidence suggests that countries of sub-Saharan Africa (SSA) are less integrated than the developed areas of East Asia, Europe and North America, and face increasing global inequality (Martell, 2008). Although SSA witnessed high rates of growth during the 2000s (almost 50% higher than the global average), the number of people living on $1.25 per day increased by 59%. Similarly, and despite its recent high growth rates, India witnessed a further 42 million people living below the absolute poverty line (Chataway et al., 2013).

1.4 Inclusive innovation reconsidered

Living in a world of technological abundance creates the moral obligation to make innovation a more inclusive and just social process. Not only in terms of the fair distribution of new goods and services which have the potential to eliminate poverty and reduce inequality, but also in terms of the social relations of innovation generation. To paraphrase Young (1990), while distributional issues of innovation are crucial to justice it would be a cardinal mistake to reduce justice to distribution. That is why inclusive innovation should be reconsidered from the point of view of a justice that is not only distributive but relational which, in turn, implies that the generation of new values through knowledge and innovation ought to be guided by non-ideal principles of justice.

However, non-ideal principles cannot only be concerned with equalising access to innovative resources. They also need to consider democratising innovation decision-making procedures. This presupposes both respect and recognition (Fraser & Honneth, 2003) of the collective endeavour of generating new knowledge and innovation. Without respect and recognition neither the generation of new products nor their distribution can be achieved in such a way as to meet the basic needs of the poor. Incorporating such needs in the innovation process requires equity of social relations and democratic participation.

I will argue in the next chapter that existing theories of justice and inclusivity are constructivist, distributional and not relational. As such, they fail to understand the non-ideal nature of justice in both the generation and distribution of innovation. Liberal egalitarianism, libertarianism, utilitarianism and the capabilities approach overwhelmingly focus on justice as fairness, private property rights, resources, social welfare and individual capabilities, but say very little about what Anderson (1999: 312) theorises as 'relations between superior and inferior persons. . . . Such unequal social relations generate inequalities in the distribution of freedoms, resources and welfare'.

In the area of innovation, inequalities are increasingly opposed by emerging social movements and public actors who promote broad egalitarian agendas for knowledge generation, R&D and innovation. Such agendas not only assert the moral worth of persons but also the importance of addressing basic human needs. In this sense, they offer a non-ideal and pragmatic interpretation of justice. Demands for equity, recognition and participation tend to be met through new models of innovation and development which challenge a range of scientific, cultural and political hierarchies. As will be pointed out in Chapter 3, despite the fact that these models differ from country to country, their mission remains the same: to enable people to stand in relations of equality to one another. Inequitable distribution of innovative products, lack of recognition of innovative communities and limited participation in innovation processes, however, can lead in the opposite direction.

A theory of justice in innovation needs to defend the contextual application of these principles, enabling equity, recognition and participation to become an evaluative framework of the global, national, regional and sectoral practices and institutions of innovation. In the case of practices and institutions which promote oppression and/or endorse discrimination through innovation, the theory will be able to offer critical insights and recommend change in a particular normative direction.

Concluding remarks

Inclusivity in innovation matters for the equalising of social relations in the generation and diffusion of novel products and processes able to satisfy basic human needs. However, there is a need for a novel political theory that articulates and defends bottom-up principles of equity, recognition and participation against existing theories of justice and their extension to the field of global innovation. In what follows, I will critically review theories of distributive justice such as liberal egalitarianism, libertarianism, utilitarianism and the capability approach in order to clear up any possible doubt that their extension to innovation is implausible and should be rejected.

References

Anderson, E. S. (1999) 'What Is the Point of Equality?', *Ethics*, Vol.109, No.2, pp. 287–337.

Arocena, R. and Sutz, J. (2003) 'Inequality and Innovation as Seen from the South', *Technology in Society*, Vol.25, pp. 171–182.

Arrow, K. T. (1997) 'Invaluable Goods', *Journal of Economic Literature*, Vol.35, No.2, pp. 757–765.

Barry, B. (1998) 'International Society from a Cosmopolitan Perspective', in D. Mapel and T. Nardin (eds.), *International Society: Diverse Ethical Perspectives*, Princeton, NJ: Princeton University Press.

Barry, B. (2005) *Why Social Justice Matters*, Cambridge: Polity Press.

Beitz, C. R. (1999) *Political Theory and International Relations*, Princeton, NJ: Princeton University Press.

Beitz, C. R. (2008) 'Human Rights as a Common Concern', in T. Brooks (ed.), *The Global Justice Reader*, Oxford: Blackwell.

Brock, G. (2009) *Global Justice: A Cosmopolitan Account*, Oxford: Oxford University Press.

Buchanan, A., Cole, T. and Keohane, R. O. (2011) 'Justice in the Diffusion of Innovation', *The Journal of Political Philosophy*, Vol.19, No.3, pp. 306–332.

Caney, S. (2005) *Justice beyond Borders: A Global Political Theory*, Oxford: Oxford University Press.

Chataway, J., Hanlin, R. and Kaplinsky, R. (2013) 'Inclusive Innovation: An Architecture for Policy Development', *IKD Working Paper No.65*, The Open University. Available at: www.sussex.ac.uk/webteam/gateway/file.php?name=kaplinsky-chataway-hanlin-framing-policy-for-inclusive-innovation-ikd-dp.pdf&site=25 [accessed 24 January 2018].

Chataway, J., Hanlin, R. and Kaplinsky, R. (2014) 'Inclusive Innovation: An Architecture for Policy Development', *Innovation and Development*, Vol.4, No.1, pp. 33–54.

Cohen, G. A. (2003) 'Facts and Principles', *Philosophy and Public Affairs*, Vol.31, pp. 211–245.

Cohen, J. and Sabel, C. (2006) 'Extra Rempublicam Nulla Justitia?', *Philosophy and Public Affairs*, Vol.34, No.2, pp. 145–175.

Cozzens, S. (2007) 'Distributive Justice in Science and Technology Policy', *Science and Public Policy*, Vol.34, No.2, pp. 85–94.

Cozzens, S. and Kaplinsky, R. (2009) 'Innovation, Poverty and Inequality: Cause, Coincidence or Co-Evolution?', in B.-A. Lundvall, K. J. Joseph, C. Chaminade and J. Vang (eds.), *Handbook of Innovation Systems and Developing Countries: Building Domestic Capabilities in a Global Setting*, Cheltenham and Northampton: Edward Elgar.

Cozzens, S. and Sutz, J. (2012) *Innovation in Informal Settings: A Research Agenda*, Ottawa: IDRC.

Cozzens, S. and Sutz, J. (2014) 'Innovation in Informal Settings', *Innovation and Development*, Vol.4, pp. 5–31.

De Haan, A. (1997) 'Poverty and Social Exclusion: A Comparison of Debates on Deprivation', *Working Paper No.2*, Poverty Research Unit at Sussex, Brighton: University of Sussex.

Dosi, G., Marengo, L. and Pasquali, C. (2006) 'How Much Should Society Fuel the Greed of Innovators? On the Relations between Appropriability, Opportunities and Rates of Innovation', *Research Policy*, Vol.35, pp. 1110–1121.

Edquist, C. (1997) *Systems of Innovation: Technologies, Institutions and Organisations*, London: Pinter.

Eubanks, V. (2007) 'Popular Technology: Exploring Inequality in the Information Economy', *Science and Public Policy*, Vol.34, No.2, pp. 127–138.

Figueiredo, J. B. and De Haan, A. (eds.) (1998) *Social Exclusion: An ILO Perspective*, Geneva: International Labour Organisation.

Foster, C. and Heeks, R. (2013) 'Conceptualising Inclusive Innovation: Modifying Systems of Innovation Framework to Understand Diffusion of New Technology to Low-Income Consumers', *European Journal of Development Research*, Vol.25, No.3, pp. 333–355.

Fosu, A. K. (2011) 'Growth, Inequality, and Poverty Reduction in Developing Countries: Recent Global Evidence' BWPI Working Paper 147, Available at: http://www.un.org/esa/socdev/egms/docs/2011/Growth-Inequality.pdf [accessed 25 April 2018]

Fraser, N. and Honneth, A. (2003) *Redistribution or Recognition? A Political-Philosophical Exchange*, London and New York: Verso.

Freeman, C. (1987) *Technology Policy and Economic Performance: Lessons for Japan*, London and New York: Pinter.

Freeman, C. and Soete, L. (1997) *The Economics of Industrial Innovation*, 3rd ed., London and New York: Routledge.

Gore, C. and Figueiredo, J. B. (1997) *Social Exclusion and Anti-Poverty Policy*, Geneva: International Labour Organisation.

26   *Why inclusivity in innovation matters*

Hanlon, J., Barrientos, A. and Hulme, D. (2010) *Just Give Money to the Poor*, Sterling, USA: Kumarian Press.
Heeks, R., Foster, C. and Nugroho, Y. (2015) *New Models of Inclusive Innovation for Development*, London: Routledge.
Hettne, B. (2009) *Thinking about Development*, London and New York: Zed Books.
Hickey, S. and du Toit, A. (2007) 'Adverse Incorporation, Social Exclusion and Chronic Poverty', *Working Paper No. 81*, Chronic Poverty Research Centre, University of Manchester.
Hollis, A. and Pogge, T. (2008) 'The Health Impact Fund: Making New Medicines Accessible for All'. Available at: www.incentivesforglobalhealth.org
ICSU, ISSC (2015) *Review of the Sustainable Development Goals: The Science Perspective*, Paris: International Council for Science (ICSU).
Jordan, B. (1996) *A Theory of Poverty and Social Exclusion*, Oxford: Blackwell.
Juma, C. (2013) 'Technological Innovation and Human Rights: An Evolutionary Approach', *Working Paper*, Harvard Kennedy School.
Juma, C., Fang, K., Honca, D., Huete-Pérez, J., Konde, V. and Lee, S. H. (2001) 'Global Governance of Technology: Meeting the Needs of Developing Countries', *International Journal of Technology Management*, Vol.22, Nos.7/8, pp. 629–655.
Kaplinsky, R. (2011) 'Bottom of the Pyramid Innovation and Pro-Poor Growth', *IKD Working Paper No.62*. The Open University. Available at: www.open.ac.uk/ikd/sites/www.open.ac.uk.ikd/files/files/working-papers/ikd-working-paper-62.pdf [accessed 24 January 2018].
Koivusalo, M. and Mackintosh, M. (2009) 'Global Public Action in Health and Pharmaceutical Policies: Politics and Policy Priorities', *IKD Working Paper No.45*, pp. 1–47. Available at: www.open.ac.uk/ikd/sites/www.open.ac.uk.ikd/files/files/working-papers/ikd-working-paper-45.pdf
Lundvall, B.-A. (1992) *National Systems of Innovation: Towards a Theory of Innovation and Interactive Learning*, London: Pinter.
Martell, L. (2008) 'Beck's Cosmopolitan Politics', *Contemporary Politics*, Vol.14, No.2, pp. 129–143.
Marx, K. (2000) 'The Communist Manifesto', in D. McLellan (ed.), *Karl Marx: Selected Writings*, Oxford: Oxford University Press.
Marx, K. and Engels, F. (1999) *The German Ideology*, London: Lawrence and Wishart.
Mason, A. (2004) 'Just Constraints', *British Journal of Political Science*, Vol.34, pp. 251–268.
Milanovic, B. (2016) *Global Inequality: A New Approach for the Age of Globalisation*, Cambridge, MA: Harvard University Press.
Nagel, T. (2005) 'The Problem of Global Justice', *Philosophy and Public Affairs*, Vol.33, No.2, pp. 113–147.
Nederveen Pieterse, J. (2010) *Development Theory*, London: Sage.
Nelson, R. and Winter, S. (1977) 'In Search of a Useful Theory of Innovation', *Research Policy*, Vol.6, No.1, pp. 36–76.
Nussbaum, M. C. (2000) *Women and Human Development: The Capabilities Approach*, Cambridge: Cambridge University Press.
Nussbaum, M. C. (2008) 'Capabilities as Fundamental Entitlements: Sen and Social Justice', in T. Brooks (ed.), *The Global Justice Reader*, Oxford: Blackwell.

OECD (2013) *Innovation and Inclusive Development*, Conference Discussion Report revised, February 2013. Available at: www.oecd.org/sti/inno/oecd-inclusive-innovation.pdf [accessed 24 January 2018].

O'Neill, O. (2002) 'Public Health or Clinical Ethics: Thinking beyond Borders', *Ethics and International Affairs*, Vol.16, No.2, pp. 35–45.

Onsongo, E. and Schot, J. (2017) 'Inclusive Innovation and Rapid Sociotechnical Transitions: The Case of Mobile Money in Kenya'. Available at: www.johanschot. com/wordpress/wp-content/uploads/2017/02/Onsongo.Schot_.Inclusive-Innovation-Working-Paper-6.2.17.pdf [accessed 24 January 2018].

Papaioannou, T. (2012) *Reading Hayek in the 21st Century: A Critical Inquiry into His Political Theory*, Basingstoke: Palgrave Macmillan.

Papaioannou, T. (2014) 'Innovation and Development in Search of a Political Theory of Justice', *International Journal of Technology and Globalisation*, Vol.7, No.3, pp. 179–202.

Papaioannou, T., Wield, D. and Chataway, J. (2009) 'Knowledge Ecologies and Ecosystems? An Empirically Grounded Reflection on Recent Developments in Innovation Systems Theory', *Environment and Planning C: Government and Policy*, Vol.27, No.2, pp. 319–339.

Piketty, T. (2014) *Capital in the Twenty-First Century*, Harvard: Belknap Press.

Pogge, T. W. (2002) *World Poverty and Human Rights: Cosmopolitan Responsibilities and Reforms*, Cambridge: Polity Press.

Pogge, T. W. (2008) 'Growth and Inequality: Understanding Recent Trends and Political Choices', *Dissent*, pp. 66–75. Available at: www.dissentmagazine.org/ article/?article=990 [accessed 24 January 2018].

Rawls, J. (1972) *A Theory of Justice*, Oxford: Oxford University Press.

Rodgers, G., Gore, C. and Figueiredo, J. B. (eds.) (1995) *Social Exclusion: Rhetoric, Reality, Responses*, Geneva: International Institute for Labour Studies.

Rogers, E. M. (1995) *Diffusion of Innovations*, New York: The Free Press.

Schot, J. and Steinmueller, W. E. (2016) 'Framing Innovation Policy for Transformative Change: Innovation Policy 3.0', *Science Policy Research Unit (SPRU)*, University of Sussex. Available at: www.johanschot.com/wordpress/wp-content/ uploads/2016/09/Framing-Innovation-Policy-for-Transformative-Change-Innovation-Policy-3.0-2016.pdf [accessed 24 January 2018].

Schumacher, E. F. (1973) *Small Is Beautiful: A Study of Economics as If People Mattered*, London: Blond & Briggs.

Schumpeter, J. A. (1983) *The Theory of Economic Development*, New Brunswick and London: Transaction Publishers.

Sen, A. (2000) 'Social Exclusion: Concept, Application and Scrutiny', *Social Development Papers No.1*, Office of Environment and Social Development, Asian Development Bank. Available at: www.adb.org/sites/default/files/publication/29778/ social-exclusion.pdf [accessed 24 January 2018].

Sen, A. (2009) *The Idea of Justice*, London: Penguin.

Silver, H. (1995) 'Reconceptualising Social Disadvantage: Three Paradigms of Social Exclusion', in G. Rodgers, C. Gore and J. Figueiredo (eds.), *Social Exclusion: Rhetoric, Reality, Responses*, Geneva: International Institute for Labour Studies.

Singer, H., Cooper, C., Desai, R. C., Freeman, C., Gish, O., Hill, S. and Oldham, G. (1970) *The Sussex Manifesto: Science and Technology to Developing Countries During the Second Development Decade*, New York: United Nations.

Singer, P. (2008) 'Famine, Affluence and Morality', in T. Brooks (ed.), *The Global Justice Reader*, Oxford: Blackwell.

Smith, A. (1976) *The Theory of Moral Sentiments*, Oxford: Oxford University Press.

Smith, A., Fressoli, M., Abrol, D., Around, E. and Ely, A. (2017) *Grassroots Innovation Movements*, London and New York: Routledge.

Srinivas, S. (2012) *Market Menagerie: Health and Development in Late Industrial States*, Stanford: Stanford University Press.

Timmermann, C. (2013) *Life Sciences, Intellectual Property Regimes and Global Justice*, PhD Thesis, Wageningen: University of Wageningen.

UNCTAD (2017) *New Innovation Approaches to Support the Implementation of the Sustainable Development Goals*, New York and Geneva: United Nations.

UNDP (2001) *Human Development Report 2001: Making New Technologies Work for Human Development*, Oxford and New York: Oxford University Press.

UN Millennium Project (2005) Innovation: Applying Knowledge in Development, London and Sterling, Va: Earthscan. Available at: https://www.belfercenter.org/sites/default/files/legacy/files/tf-advance2.pdf [accessed 25 April 2018]

Wolff, J. (2006) 'Models of Distributive Justice'. Available at: http://sas-space.sas.ac.uk/678/1/J_Wolff_Justice.pdf [accessed 24 January 2018].

Woodhouse, E. and Sarewitz, D. (2007) 'Science Policies for Reducing Social Inequities', *Science and Public Policy*, Vol.34, No.2, pp. 139–150.

World Bank (2010) *World Development Indicators 2010*, Washington, DC: The World Bank.

World Bank (2016) *Poverty and Shared Prosperity: Taking on Inequality*, Washington, DC: World Bank Group. Available at: https://openknowledge.worldbank.org/bitstream/handle/10986/25078/9781464809583.pdf

Young, I. M. (1990) *Justice and the Politics of Difference*, Princeton, NJ: Princeton University Press.

2 Existing theories of justice and inclusivity

In the preceding chapter I put forward two arguments: first, that the question of inclusivity in innovation matters because poverty and inequality in the 21st century are, among other things, due to new technologies which exclude the interests of low-income populations, especially in developing countries; second, that it is important to outline a theory of justice in innovation that addresses this question in terms of the moral obligation to equalise social relations in the generation and diffusion of novel technological products and services which satisfy basic human needs. Before I undertake the latter task, however, it is necessary to review critically existing cosmopolitan theories of justice in more detail in order to investigate whether they have anything to offer to the current debate about inclusive innovation. This chapter therefore focuses on liberal egalitarianism, libertarianism, utilitarianism and the capabilities approach. While this index is not necessarily exhaustive of the range of cosmopolitan arguments, it is representative of the main liberal approaches to justice. In what follows, I argue that liberal cosmopolitan theories of justice are either characterised by philosophical idealism and constructivism, or they affirm principles which ignore social relations and lack socio-political foundations. As a result, I propose moving away from liberal cosmopolitan justice towards a 'smarter' needs-based approach to inclusive innovation for development. Such an approach is predominately non-ideal and political, and understands innovation to be a relational process of transformation that is embedded in socio-economic and political structures, including capitalist production and diffusion of new technological goods and services.

2.1 Liberal egalitarianism

Liberal egalitarianism includes principles of justice at the centre of which lies the liberal notion of equality (i.e. the formal equal liberty of everyone in society). Egalitarians such as Rawls advanced equal liberty from a hypothetical 'original position' of choice of ideal principles of justice (Rawls, 1972). In order to achieve equal liberty, Rawls assumes his original position to be behind a 'veil of ignorance'. This assumption is epistemological and aims towards the construction of ideal principles of justice in abstraction from historically developed socio-economic and political conditions of capitalism. Thus, Rawls says 'no one knows his place in society, his class position or social status, nor does anyone know his fortune in the distribution of natural assets and abilities, his intelligence, strength and the like' (Rawls, 1972: 12). Rawls's original position permits him to derive two fundamental principles of justice as fairness:

1   Each person has an equal right to the most extensive scheme of equal basic liberties compatible with a similar scheme of liberties for all.
2   Social and economic inequalities are to satisfy two conditions: they must be (a) to the greatest benefit of the least advantaged members of society; and (b) attached to offices and positions open to all under conditions of fair equality of opportunity.

(Rawls, 1999b: 362)

In abstract terms, neither principle – equal liberty and the so-called difference principle – justifies innovation exclusion. In 'a well-ordered society' (Rawls, 1999b: 361), free and equal moral persons cannot be excluded from technological innovations which are to the greatest benefit of the least advantaged. Rawls's difference principle has two parts: 'Part (b) . . . has priority over part (a), so that the conditions of fair equality of opportunity are also guaranteed for everyone'.

Rawls's argument appears to have two major problems. The first is the ideal nature of 'equal liberty' and the 'difference principle'. If innovators, regulators and publics knew in advance their different place in society, class position or social status and natural talents, they might never agree to adopt Rawls's ideal principles of justice for guiding the generation and distribution of new knowledge and innovation. As I have already implied, the original position is not an empirical and historical fact but a theoretical construction that provides weak legitimacy to these ideal principles. In the non-ideal world of capitalism, innovators, regulators and publics make choices according to their social and class background, material interests and values. Such choices are not, therefore, necessarily inclusive of the worst off. Indeed the opposite is true. In the non-ideal world of capitalism, innovators, regulators and publics are involved in hierarchical relations of power which exclude the worst off and their basic needs. As will be argued later in this book, such relations manifest themselves in value chains of innovative products governed by dominant multinational companies, some of which companies totally ignore the poor and their basic needs simply because they cannot translate these into effective demand, creating profitable markets for innovative goods and services.

The second problem with the application of Rawls's theory of justice in innovation is that even if innovators, regulators and publics agreed to adopt the 'equal liberty' and the 'difference principle' as their normative framework, the latter's application to the basic structure of society would lead to unequal access of innovations and eventually to exclusion. As Cozzens (2007: 90) points out, Rawls's

> Justice as fairness could be incorporated into current S&T policies without demanding change in general rationales or goals, just a shift in practices. The policies could aim both to make the pie bigger through encouraging commercial activities and consciously work to achieve justice as fairness by making sure that the least advantaged benefit through programmes oriented to public goods.

As Cozzens goes on to argue, however, this is neither 'inclusive utilitarianism' nor 'better life strategy'. Rather it is a theory that, in concrete terms, promotes exclusion in the social processes of innovation. To put it another way, Rawls's theory of justice fails to equalise relations between the worst-off and the better-off members of society, which results in the reproduction of unjust inequality and oppression in the generation and use of novel goods and services that satisfy human needs.

It might be argued that the main rationale behind Rawls's theory of justice is to maintain a morally acceptable level of fairness without providing negative incentives for entrepreneurship and innovation-led growth. The acceptance of social and economic inequalities which are to the greatest benefit of the least advantaged implies that incentives for innovation such as IPRs can be justified in the case of developing new technological products and processes which do not leave the least advantaged worst off. In the area of health, for example, patents for developing new drugs which benefit the worst off can be justified on Rawlsian grounds. The worst off, however, might then have unequal access to these biopharmaceutical innovations and thus face relative (as opposed to absolute) exclusivity.

Despite these problems, contemporary cosmopolitan theorists such as Beitz (2010) and Pogge (2002) propose the extension of Rawlsian egalitarianism to a global level. Their argument is that modern societies are not self-contained but rather have relations of different kinds with persons, groups or societies beyond their borders. Therefore, according to Beitz (2010: 86), 'If the societies of the world are now to be conceived as open, fully interdependent systems, the world as a whole would fit the description of a scheme of social co-operation and the argument for the two principles would apply, a fortiori, at the global level'. Although, in *The Law of Peoples*, Rawls (1999a) explicitly rejects the cosmopolitan relationship between 'global and domestic' political theory, Beitz and Pogge insist that a global egalitarian theory of justice can only be Rawlsian in its principles. As has been argued elsewhere (Papaioannou et al., 2009) this is a somewhat problematic position since it ignores that what matters for Rawls is justice within peoples' societies rather than the well-being of individuals.

Indeed, Rawls's theory is primarily concerned with the basic structure of peoples' societies rather than furthering the standard of living of individual persons. According to Rawls (1999a), the final political end of peoples' societies is to become fully just and stable. This serves to illustrate the contrast between his theory and cosmopolitans' view of justice. Criticising the latter, Rawls (ibid.: 119) argues that:

> The ultimate concern of a cosmopolitan view is the well-being of individuals and not the justice of societies. According to that view there is still a question concerning the need for further global distribution, even after each domestic society has achieved internally just institutions.

Rawls's argument implies a 'reasonable pluralism' that does not allow the extension of his 'difference principle' to the global level. This pluralism is founded upon the 'Law of Peoples' rather than upon universal liberal principles of justice as fairness. As Rawls (ibid.: 85–86) says,

> The principles of justice for the basic structure of a liberal democratic society are not . . . fully general principles. They do not apply . . . to basic structures of all societies. And also do not hold for the Law of Peoples, which is autonomous.

Thus, at a global level, Rawls seems to prioritise formalism over cosmopolitanism. This is clearly illustrated by his pluralist distinction between two kinds of peoples: 'liberal peoples' and 'decent peoples'. The first kind of peoples is liberal and has developed formal constitutional regimes, while the second is illiberal but has respect for the rule of law. Liberal peoples and decent peoples constitute what Rawls calls the 'Society of Peoples' that is bound by the 'Law of Peoples'. As he (ibid.: 3) explains,

> By the 'Law of Peoples' I mean a particular political conception of rights and justice that applies to the principles and norms of international law and practice. I shall use the term 'Society of Peoples' to mean all those peoples who follow the ideals and principles of the Law of Peoples in their mutual relations.

In Rawls's account, the ideals and principles of the Law of Peoples are chosen by representatives of liberal peoples in a second-level original position from which 'the only alternatives for the parties to pick from . . . are formulations of the Law of Peoples' (ibid.: 40).

Certainly contemporary cosmopolitan theorists such as Beitz and Pogge, despite their endorsement of justice as fairness, are in direct disagreement with Rawls's argument. As Beitz (2010: 92) stresses,

> Rawls' passing concern for the law of nations seems to miss the point of international justice altogether. In an interdependent world, conflicting principles of social justice to national societies has the effect of taxing poor nations so that others may benefit from living in just regimes. The two principles, so constructed, might justify a wealthy nation's denying aid to needy peoples if the aid could be used domestically to promote a more nearly just regime.

Indeed, Beitz believes that domestic principles of justice should be consistent with principles of justice for the entire global structure. According to his theory, such global principles can only be the Rawlsian 'equal liberty' and 'difference principle'. As such, they can only be derived from an international original position and from behind a veil of ignorance that extends to all matters of national citizenship.

The extension of 'equal liberty' and the 'difference principle' to the global basic structure by liberal cosmopolitans has provided the normative basis for theorists such as Pogge (2005) and Buchanan et al. (2011) to develop specific institutional proposals for dealing with the issue of unjust inequality in the global generation and diffusion of innovation. To begin with Pogge (2005) focuses on one crucial area of innovation: global health. He therefore suggests an institutional proposal of establishing a Health Impact Fund (HIF) which aims to address two aspects of global health: the lack of equal access to essential medicines and the failure to develop innovative drugs for the poor. Both of these are due to the problem of a lack of market demand in low-income countries (Prahalad, 2005). As a solution, Pogge proposes an alternative IPR system (which he calls the 'Patent 2 option') which operates in parallel to the current IPR system (which he calls the 'Patent 1 option'). While this requires innovators to make public all information about their innovation, it also makes them eligible for reward from an international HIF in proportion to the positive impact of their innovation in increasing health and decreasing poverty. According to Hollis and Pogge (2008: 9),

> To be eligible to register a product under the HIF reward scheme, a company must hold a patent (on the product) from one of a set of patent offices specified by the HIF. It can then register its product with

the HIF and will then be rewarded on the basis of the product's global health impact in its first ten years following marketing approval.

Although the HIF mechanism was designed to resolve the 'innovation-justice trade off' and promote proactive or creative equality, it fails to do so in several crucial respects. Chief among these is that Pogge's global institutional proposal is based on the profit-incentives argument. Paraphrasing Cohen (2008), this might be described as follows: when innovative people take home modest pay, they innovate less than they otherwise might, as a result of which relatively poor and badly off people are worse off than they would be if the exercise of innovation talent were better rewarded. The problem with the profit-incentives argument is its claim that the profit incentives for innovation which produce inequality can be justified on the grounds that they make badly off people better off. In Pogge's proposal, the more positive the impact of innovations on increasing health and decreasing poverty, the higher the reward for their innovators from an international HIF.

Following Cohen (2008), it might further be argued that the profit-incentives argument that underpins the HIF fails to pass the interpersonal test. Indeed, the profit-incentives argument can justify inequality only in a society in which interpersonal relations lack a communal character. In a cosmopolitan society in which neo-Rawlsians envisage citizens justifying to one another their common institutions of justice as fairness, the profit-incentives argument of innovation is problematical. In addition, the key question of whether significant inequalities are required for optimal innovative motivation can be answered from the point of view of internal gains to innovation performance. According to Cohen (ibid.: 53), 'the desire to achieve, to shine, and, yes, to outshine, can elicit enormous effort even in the absence of pecuniary motivation'. These represent alternative non-profit incentives (rather than non-incentives) which, as has been pointed out elsewhere (Papaioannou, 2011), can be based on a conception of basic human needs. The fact that Pogge's HIF ignores the existence of such non-profit incentives for innovation and the communal relations within which such incentives can be promoted is one crucial shortcoming of his theory.

Another shortcoming is, of course, that the HIF is limited to one kind of innovation; namely health. This narrowness has been criticised by non-Rawlsian cosmopolitans such as Buchanan et al. (2011) who are concerned about basic economic and social inequality. In addition, the HIF has been criticised for its voluntariness. As Buchanan et al. (ibid.: 20) point out:

> Drug companies could decide, case-by-case, whether to invoke Patent 1 or Patent 2 protections. The voluntary nature of Patent 2 is a double sword, since firms might never invoke the Patent 2 option. Never

invoked, Patent 2 would be like unfinished monuments in the desert: testimonies to failed ambition. The big question about Patent 2 therefore is whether firms will invoke it.

According to Buchanan et al. (ibid.: 325), the answer to this question depends on the credibility of the reward promise:

> For the promise to be sufficiently credible to induce drug producers to forgo the known benefits of the Patent 1 option, two things must be true. First, drug producers must have confidence that the promised funds will be available. . . . We call this the *funding assumption*. Second, the firms must have confidence that the procedure for identifying the disease burden reduced by drug, and therefore the patent 2 rewards due to drug companies, will be reliable and fair. Call this the *reliability assumption*.

They go on to insist that none of these assumptions are true. First, the *funding assumption* is not credible because international funding pledges are not trustworthy. Second, the *reliability assumption* is problematic because of the epistemological and methodological difficulty of reaching agreement on reliable measurements of the impact of a particular drug on a disease.

In order to avoid the narrowness and voluntariness of Pogge's HIF, Buchanan et al. (ibid.) propose a new institution: the Global Institute for Justice in Innovation (GIJI). Rather than solely health, their concern is the impediment to the diffusion of innovation in general. As a result, non-Rawlsians such as Buchanan et al. (ibid.: 9) propose 'to modify the IPR regime in a way that preserves its valuable functions while remedying or at least significantly ameliorating its institutional failures'. Specifically, they argue that the GIJI would be an organisation designed to construct and implement a set of rules and policies governing the just diffusion of innovations. This organisation would be similar to the WTO and would (ibid.: 9):

> Encourage the creation of useful innovations, for example through prizes and grants for justice-promoting innovations and through offering extended patent life for innovations that have a positive impact on justice. But its major efforts would be directed towards the wider and faster diffusion in order to ameliorate extreme deprivations and reduce their negative impact on basic political and economic inequalities.

Non-Rawlsians insist that the most important asset of GIJI would be the 'licensing option', i.e. the option to authorise compulsory licensing of slowly diffusing innovations. Another asset would be the 'compensation option' offered through GIJI rather than through royalties from the sales of licensed products.

Although both options are important, they do not transcend the profit-incentives argument. Buchanan et al. fail to think in egalitarian terms outside the current IPR system. The latter promotes what Cohen (2008: 53) describes as 'a population of talented people each of whom is a unique moral hero' rather than an egalitarian global society. In this sense, neither the profit-incentive for useful innovations nor the compulsory licensing of slowly diffusing innovations is able to resolve the 'innovation-justice trade off'. But even if we assumed they were, they would still face serious operational problems. Encouraging useful innovations through grants and/ or authorising compulsory licensing would presuppose that GIJI receives political support from its member states and therefore becomes not only legal but also a legitimate global entity.

It might be argued that these presuppositions do not exist in the non-Rawlsian proposal. First, as Buchanan et al. (ibid.) confess, it is difficult for powerful developed states to provide political support for a global institution that might authorise compulsory licensing of innovation-creating firms' products. Even if positive incentives for developed countries and their firms to support GIJI exist (such as more rapid diffusion of innovation, acceleration of economic development worldwide, less arbitrary compulsory licensing procedures, etc.), there are also negative incentives (such as reduction of immediate profits, loss of economic and political power, etc) and the latter are stronger than the former. Non-Rawlsians overlook the fact that innovative firms in sectors such as health spend millions of dollars from their profits to lobby governments in favour of their economic interests (Papaioannou, 2011).

Second, even if powerful developed states did provide support for GIJI, they would do so on the grounds of their own set of rules and principles of justice. Buchanan et al. (2011) seem to overlook the material interests and power relations that exist between dominant developed states such as the US and developing countries (Rosenberg, 1994; Callinicos, 2002). Thus they propose global political institutions such as the WTO or the IMF as models for GIJI. In fact, these top-down institutions constitute nothing more than arenas of the global struggles of material interests and power between developed and developing countries, and it is these struggles that undermine the political basis for GIJI. No matter how important non-Rawlsian cosmopolitanism is as a theory of justice in innovation and development, global cosmopolitan politics may not be a plausible way of pursuing such a theory. This critique of Buchanan et al. (2011) echoes Martell's recent critique of cosmopolitanism in which he argues that 'cosmopolitan ethics may require non-cosmopolitan politics' (Martell, 2011: 621). This implies a conflict approach to politics of global justice in innovation and development. A conflict approach goes beyond Anglo-American and other Western traditions of liberal cosmopolitanism and towards considering the different social and economic contexts in which developmental processes take place. I will come back to Martell's argument later, but first I shall move on to libertarianism and examine whether it has anything to offer in the debate about inclusive innovation.

2.2 Libertarianism

The tradition of libertarianism includes ideal principles of justice which are founded upon the notion of inviolable individual rights. Thus, Nozick (1974: ix) insists that 'Individuals have rights, and there are things no person or group may do to them (without violating their rights)'. Libertarians hold that social redistribution violates individual rights and especially the right to self-ownership, for example: 'Every person is morally entitled to full private property in his person and powers. This means that each person has an extensive set of moral rights . . . over the use and fruits of his body and capacities' (Cohen & Graham, 1990: 25). On the bases of self-ownership and the moral inviolability of persons, libertarians construct principles of justice which presuppose a minimal state. For instance, Nozick (1974: 151) claims that

> If the world was wholly just, the following inductive definition would exhaustively cover the subject of justice in holdings.
>
> 1 A person who acquires a holding in accordance with the principle of justice in acquisition is entitled to that holding.
> 2 A person who acquires a holding in accordance with the principle of justice in transfer, from someone else entitled to the holding, is entitled to the holding.
> 3 No one is entitled to a holding except by (repeated) applications of 1 and 2.

Libertarians consider themselves to be in the opposite side of liberal egalitarianism. For this reason, Nozick (ibid.) attacks Rawls for focusing justice on the basic structure of society and for failing to respect the separateness of persons by redistributing the economic and social goods that flow from their own natural goods to those whom nature has endowed less generously (Dunn, 1996). This means that the libertarians can only address concerns about exclusive innovation from the standpoint of inviolable individual rights. Nozick argues that each person is morally entitled to his/her own body and powers. From this it follows that each person also possesses a moral right over ownership of his/her own innovative abilities. No one is morally justified to interfere with the self-ownership of each person without his/her consent.

Nozick's argument places primary value on private property rights. Only when individuals are able to exercise such rights (entitlements to holdings) in a free market can libertarian justice be achieved. In what Nozick terms a 'minimal state', government functions should be limited to those that protect private property owners against force, theft and fraud, and to enforcing contracts. Nozick's libertarian argument might be considered to be particularly hostile towards the idea of inclusive innovation as it provides moral justification for IPR. By recognising that each individual is entitled to his/her talents and abilities, Nozick justifies each innovator's acquisition of the benefits of whatever innovative products and processes have been generated on the basis of those talents and abilities. Application of the entitlement theory of justice to innovation would thus lead to the following statement: If I own an innovation, then Principle 1 tells me how the innovation came to be owned; Principle 2 says that I am free to transfer my innovation as I wish; Principle 3 tells me what to do in the case of violation of Principles 1 and 2.

Nozick's entitlement theory implies that if people's current innovations and related benefits are justly acquired (if they are not stolen but are based on talent and ability, for example), then just distribution can only take place in a free market. People have the right to sell and to buy innovations, benefiting from exchange. The state is not morally justified in intervening in order to redistribute the benefits of innovations to naturally disadvantaged or less creative people. Only the owners of innovations can decide on such distribution. Although Nozick derives most of his arguments from the Lockean theory of property, he goes beyond this in leaving no space for inclusive innovation policies at all. He believes that his principles are more consistent with our intuitions than social redistributive principles.

Although the Nozickian libertarian argument of justice has not been systematically extended to the global level, one thing is clear: it provides justification for global innovation policy mechanisms such as the TRIPS Agreement which aim to protect the private ownership of scientific knowledge and innovation. By requiring the standardisation of IPR law among all WTO members by 1 January 2005, TRIPS formalised the exclusion of low-income countries and individuals from technological innovation. Clearly, Nozick's theory is consistent with the rationale behind TRIPS. Indeed, as Cozzens (2007: 87) points out, 'The principles of acquisition and transfer figure in one of the hottest intellectual property debates of current science and technology policy, one connected to the sense of justice in relationships between rich and poor countries'.

In fact, libertarians fail to recognise knowledge and innovation as social relational processes. In this sense, they also disagreed with the so-called Doha Declaration (WTO, 2001) according to which the least developed countries would not be obliged to implement TRIPS until 1 January 2016 and would retain the option of the compulsory licensing of drugs (Westerhaus & Castro, 2006). Nozick discusses patents explicitly in his *Anarchy, State and Utopia*, arguing that 'An inventor's patent does not deprive others of an object which would not exist if not for the inventor' (Nozick, 1974: 182). This argument clearly provides justification for the absolute implementation of TRIPS and demands its enforcement. Countries such as the US and multinational companies (MNCs) have used the libertarian argument to challenge morally and legally countries such as Brazil and South Africa for their granting of compulsory licenses. In the name of absolute liberty and private property rights, the global regime of IPRs has had a negative impact on the pharmaceutical products of developing countries with crucial consequences for the poor (Ryan, 2009). Innovative drugs and therapies have become more expensive as a consequence of courts' enforcement of TRIPS (Médecins San Frontières, 2011). In short, the restriction of reverse engineering of drugs under patents and the inevitable cost of essential medicines brought several developing countries, including India and Brazil, close to health crisis.

2.3 Utilitarianism

Both liberal egalitarianism and libertarianism constitute responses to utilitarianism. The latter claims that people ought to act in such a way that they produce the greatest happiness for the greatest number of the members of society. Utilitarianism is in a consequentialist tradition of political morality in the sense that

> It demands of anyone who condemns something as morally wrong that they show who is wronged, e.g. they must show how someone's life is made worse off. Likewise, consequentialism says that something is morally good only if it makes someone's life better off.
>
> (Kymlicka, 1990: 10)

Certainly there are different versions of utilitarianism, including hedonistic utilitarianism, welfarist utilitarianism and preference utilitarianism. However, utilitarianism, especially in the hedonistic version advanced by Bentham (1970) and Mill (1937), essentially conceives happiness as a sum of pleasures. Pleasure is morally good and pain is morally bad (Raphael, 1994). According to Dworkin (1977: 160), utilitarianism is a goal-based theory concerned with the welfare or well-being of each individual. As such, it is competing with rights-based theories of justice, including Rawls's liberal egalitarianism and Nozick's libertarianism. For utilitarians, rights are simply legal obligations which contribute to maximisation of the aggregate utility (Lyons, 1984). Bentham (1970: 11–12) defines utility as the 'principle which approves or disapproves of every action whatsoever, according to the tendency which it appears to have to augment or diminish the happiness of the party whose interest is in question'. This principle is considered to be the only one that gives equal weight to the competing interests of different individual actors in a liberal society (Hare, 1982).

As a theory, utilitarianism competes with both liberal egalitarianism and libertarianism in addressing the question of the fair distribution of innovation. Specifically, within utilitarianism, concerns about innovation exclusion might be dealt with from the standpoint of maximisation of aggregate utility or well-being. This implication that judgements might be made on the grounds of overall consequences and welfare constitutes what Rawls (1982) would call one rational good. For utilitarians, therefore, innovation exclusion is not intrinsically immoral. Indeed, the exclusion of people from particular innovations under certain circumstances of aggregate utility maximisation is justified. It is true, of course, that utilitarianism epistemologically fails to provide 'objective' measures of aggregate utility while, at the same time, totally neglecting individual rights and freedoms. A combination of that has a serious impact on addressing innovation exclusion as a concern of justice. In essence, individuals can be excluded from technological innovations as long as these innovations increase total well-being.

Utilitarians assume that by increasing benefits to society as a whole, new technological products and processes will also benefit each individual. However, they never raise the question of fair access to innovation. For utilitarians, the primary distributive mechanism of new products and processes is the market – no matter if the state consistently invests in R&D for maximising utility or not. Indeed as Cozzens (2007: 88) confirms:

> On the one hand, utilitarian principles of justice are not inherently distributive: well-being could increase for everyone, or large gains in well-being for some could outweigh losses by others; both situations are morally justified under utilitarianism as long as total well-being is growing. On the other hand, if inequality creates negative consequences that reduce total well-being . . . then actions that increase inequality would be morally wrong in utilitarian terms.

This second tenet of a utilitarian approach to inequality has provided the foundation for extending principles of utility to the global level. Peter Singer

(2008: 388), a well-known utilitarian thinker, begins with the assumption that, at global level, 'suffering and death from lack of food, shelter and medical care are bad'. This assumption derives from Bentham's theory that suggests we all ought to be working towards increasing the total balance of happiness over that of suffering and misery. Consistent with this theory, Singer (2008: 392) proposes the following principle: 'we ought, morally, to be working full-time to relieve great suffering of the sort that occurs as a result of famine or other disasters'. This utilitarian principle has implications for innovation. New technological products and services ought to be generated and distributed in such a way as to maximise global happiness and minimise suffering. However, because its main focus is on aggregate utility, Singer's utilitarian principle does not address the question of the unjust exclusion of disadvantaged poor people and places from innovation. Aggregate utility is unable to guarantee that the fruits of science, technology and innovation are equally shared by both advantaged and disadvantaged people. In fact, the utilitarian approach to global innovation promotes inequality and injustice in social relations as it has no interest in inclusion and equality as long as global utility can be maximised. Maximisation of global utility is, of course, difficult to measure. Utilitarians use economic growth as a general indicator for global utility but fail to account for its impact on individuals and their lives, especially in developing countries.

2.4 Capabilities

Compared to liberal egalitarianism, libertarianism and utilitarianism, the capabilities tradition of justice is relatively new. In the *Tanner Lectures on Human Values*, Sen (1980) asserts that what matters in the discussion of social justice is not the question 'Why equality?' but the question 'Equality of what?' It is answering the latter that provides the currency of Senian justice: in other words, capability. The capability approach shifts the focus from the basic structure of society to the basic freedoms of people. Sen is critical of Rawlsian, libertarian and utilitarian principles because in his view they become central issues in judging resource-based distributional equity. In this sense, he suggests, they contain an element of 'fetishism' (ibid.). He believes resources are merely the means by which people can be offered the freedom to choose different kinds of lives. As Sen (ibid.: 18) explains:

> Justice cannot be indifferent to the lives that people can actually live. The importance of human lives, experiences and realisations cannot be supplanted by information about institutions that exist and the rules that operate. . . . We have reason to be interested . . . in the freedoms that we actually have to choose between different kinds of lives.

This is what the notion of capability refers to: each individual's actual freedom to achieve the functioning he/she values (i.e. the leading of an autonomous and meaningful life).

Sen arrives at the notion of capability partly through his critical assessment of Rawlsian primary goods. Sen's dissatisfaction with the concept of Rawlsian primary goods is founded upon the realisation that individuals are differently capable of converting these into well-being or welfare due to variations in a range of factors, including biology, physical environment and social conditions. For example, disabled and non-disabled people cannot achieve the same level of well-being with the same amount of primary goods. Primary goods as such, therefore, do not matter; they cannot (and should not) be thought of as the currency of egalitarian justice (Cohen, 1989). What matters is what individuals are able to do with them. For Sen the ultimate concern is not primary goods as such but capabilities, and these are the result of relations between persons, goods, physical environment and social conditions. Capabilities thus imply the importance of the dimension of freedom in human lives.

The distributive objective of the capability approach is to guarantee all individuals access to the basic abilities required for the achievement of essential functionings. By so doing, no one would fall below the relevant baseline into what Sen calls a state of 'capability deprivation'. Above that baseline it seems that individuals bear responsibility for their choice of non-essential functionings. Although Sen prioritises freedom over responsibility, the latter seems important if we are to understand one crucial aspect of the capability approach: individuals who have the capability to achieve essential functionings but choose not to do so, or individuals who prefer to choose certain non-essential functionings (and who cannot then justify and sustain complaints about their failure to achieve essential functionings). As these individuals do not lack the necessary capabilities, there is no reason for them to complain or to transfer resources from those who have chosen essential functionings to those who have chosen non-essential functionings. Even though Sen never takes a clear position on this issue, he does defend a substantive freedom of choice that is impossible to separate from responsibility (Sen, 1980: 19):

> Freedom to choose gives us the opportunity to decide what we should do, but with that opportunity comes the responsibility for what we do – to the extent that they are chosen actions. Since a capability is the power to do something, the accountability that emanates from ability – that power – is a part of the capability perspective.

Certainly, to find out how many of an individual's functionings are a result of his/her choice and how many a result of unchosen circumstances, we would need to know details about that person's situation. And collecting data about a person raises a number of ethical issues, including what Wolff (1998: 97) regards as 'shameful revelation' i.e. 'one may find certain facts about oneself shameful, and not wish to reveal them' (ibid.: 113). Shameful revelation can lead to lower respect-standing and by so doing undermine egalitarian ethos. The capability approach does not demand investigation into the achievement and failure of one's own essential functionings. That is to say, we are not required to admit we are a failure because we find it difficult to achieve essential functionings, when there is no difficulty for other, equally capable, individuals.

In Sen's theory, the concept of responsibility includes the element of voluntariness. Individuals are responsible for the non-essential functionings they have voluntarily chosen (from n-tuples) as capable actors. In fact, Sen assumes responsibility exists in every individual choice. For this reason he insists that 'In dealing with responsible adults, it is more appropriate to see the claims of individuals on the society (or the demands of equity or justice) in terms of *freedom to achieve* rather than *actual achievements*' (Sen, 1995: 148). Although freedom as such is not an absolute value in Sen's theory, it is a value of primary importance or fundamental value. Indeed freedom is always the bottom line of everything. According to Fleurbaey (2006: 300) 'Typically, even when freedom is deemed important one would still look at achievements as well'. Achievements constitute consequences of the capability approach. As such, they cannot be totally ignored by Sen's evaluative system.

The components of responsibility and freedom within the capability approach make it attractive to those who defend global justice in innovation. Certainly, Sen (1999, 2009) is more interested in development than in innovation. This is because specific types of innovation are simply means of development and not ends in themselves. In so arguing, I do not deny that some innovations 'just happen'. Rather I emphasise the instrumental character of specific or targeted innovations in areas such as new life sciences and biotechnology for improving human well-being. For Sen, it seems, such innovations can substantially connect to capabilities (for example to health and food) and thereby to specific functionings that people value. His theory of justice is not about guiding the establishment of just global institutions but about guiding practical reasoning and ways of reducing injustice in development.

In contrast to liberal egalitarian, libertarian and utilitarian cosmopolitans who promote global institutional design and social structure guided by universal principles of justice, Sen's capability theory is context dependent. Development should not be seen as a global process of innovation-led growth and technological advance. Rather, it should be seen as a global process of freedom that, according to Sen (1999: 3), 'requires the removal of major sources of unfreedom: poverty as well as tyranny, poor economic opportunities as well as systematic social deprivation, neglect of public facilities as well as intolerance or overactivity of repressive states'. For Sen, freedom is both the primary end and the principal means of development. People ought to be capable of freely choosing the kind of life they (have reason to) value. In this sense, Sen proposes a specific evaluative system as a solution to the problem of global exclusion; namely the capability evaluative system. His proposal addresses 'the need to assess the requirements of development in terms of removing the unfreedoms from which the members of society may suffer' (Sen, 1999: 33).

Sen's capability evaluative system might be seen as a public policy tool that uses the metric of capabilities to identify unjust inequalities in global development. Capabilities as such are

> sets of vectors of functionings. . . . A functioning may be any kind of action performed, or state achieved, by an individual, and may *a priori* cover anything that pertains to the full description of the individual's life. Therefore, such a description may be done by a list or 'vector' (or '*n-tuple*') of functionings.
>
> (Fleurbaey, 2006: 300)

Indeed, as Fleurbaey (ibid.) notes, Sen's reason for prioritising capabilities over functionings is that by focusing only on achievements, one would miss the dimension of freedom in human life. For example, an individual life of great achievement in technological innovation and development is less great if it exists in a totalitarian state which offers little or no freedom. This, however, does not imply that freedom is an absolute value in Sen's system but that it is of primary importance. As Fleurbaey (ibid.: 305) points out: 'Typically, even when freedom is deemed important, one would still look at achievements as well'.

Certainly, the capability evaluative system has received various critiques (Clark, 2006) regarding the problem of disagreement about the valuation of capabilities (Beitz, 1986), the high informational requirements of the system (Alkire, 2002), and the paternalistic move towards determining capabilities for developing societies and systems (Jagger, 2006; Stewart, 2001). However, despite this criticism, the system has been endorsed by global policy organisations in the area of innovation and development, including the UN, the WB and even the IMF (Nederveen Pieterse, 2010). The metric of capabilities has also been applied in the human development index and used in various measurements (Anand & van Hees, 2006; Anand et al., 2007). For instance, a *Report by the Commission on the Measurement of Economic*

Performance and Social Progress clearly suggests shifting emphasis from measuring economic production to measuring people's well-being, highlighting that 'quality of life depends on people's objective condition and capabilities' (Stiglitz et al., 2008).

The key question we need to consider here is whether the capability evaluative system resolves the problem of exclusion in technological innovation and development. Is it plausible to say that avoiding basic capability deprivation at a global level can lead to more inclusive innovation and growth? Given that equalisation of basic capabilities such as, for instance, life and bodily health can provide incentives for more inclusive health innovations, the answer is in the affirmative. However, these need to be non-profit incentives if basic capabilities are to be equalised in low-income regions such as East Asia, Latin America and sub-Saharan Africa. While Sen and Nussbaum challenge the notion of universalism through their process approach, they say little about the institutional preconditions for achieving equality of basic capabilities in low-income developing regions. For example, is the current IPR system conducive to equalising basic capabilities of life and bodily health through equally accessible health innovation? And if that is the case, what is the impact of such equalisation on social relations and basic human needs?

It might be argued that the most crucial problem of the capability evaluative system is that it relies overwhelmingly on cosmopolitan politics and global institutions for its implementation, and recent analysis at an empirical sociological level indicates no basis for such politics. According to Martell (2011), in a number of cases, including that of global negotiations over trade, cosmopolitanism is undermined by the clashing material interests of powerful countries such as the US. In addition, the rise of populism in the US and Europe in 2016 and 2017 is bound to exacerbate the weakness of liberal cosmopolitanism as a moral and political doctrine of global justice. From this it follows that the capabilities solution to the global problem of exclusive innovation and development might best be implemented by non-cosmopolitan means. As Martell (ibid.: 632) states:

> This does not rule out cosmopolitanism. It means pursuing cosmopolitan ends through non-cosmopolitan approaches. Clashing material interests suggest one needs to find non-cosmopolitan politics for cosmopolitan goals. Continuing to pursue cosmopolitan means which evidence casts doubt upon may undermine cosmopolitan ends. It is better to find an alternative route.

As far as innovation and development are concerned, it might be argued that one alternative route to inclusivity is public action and campaigning for just redistributive systems and a politics of development that equalise social relations and meet basic social needs. In the next chapters I will defend this 'smarter' approach to justice in innovation and development, providing further theoretical and empirical arguments. For the time being, allow me simply to clarify the basic terms. First, although the notion of 'public' tends to be associated with the state, in the context of political theory 'the public' is used to describe citizens' participation in social and political processes. In this sense, as Mackintosh (1992: 4) points out, the 'concept of "public action" . . . is considerably wider than the actions of the state', extending to purposive collective action for public (or private) ends. Second, the term 'campaigning' can be defined as an organised public (or private) action towards a particular moral and political goal.

The global sphere of public action and campaigning includes a variety of organisations and movements. These include non-governmental organisations (NGOs); alter-globalisation movements and networks of global innovation users; South-South alliances with developing countries; and the G77 groups of developing countries in the UN. All these actors are critical of neo-liberalism, promoting the establishment of just systems of social relations and challenging the content of innovation and development policies. Third, the concept of 'need' can be described as a claim of a fundamental human desire (as opposed to a claim of preference or benefit). As Wolff (2009: 215) points out, 'Needs are always needs for something. But for what? Presumably for the elements of a flourishing life'. It might be said that the most basic elements of a flourishing life are the same for all human beings and their societies. These elements are both natural (life, nutrition, health, etc.) and social (absence of oppression, political freedom, housing, education, etc.). Universal natural and social basic needs are interrelated. For instance, health is often determined by education and housing. The interrelation between natural and social basic needs should be the basis for a new relational theory of justice in innovation and development. In the next two chapters, I will argue that this relational theory can be derived directly from global public action and campaigning for justice and innovation.

Concluding remarks

Existing liberal cosmopolitan theories of justice tend to provide ideal accounts of what shape freedom and equality ought to take in innovation and development. Such accounts clearly fail to tackle the problem of unjust social relations at a global level, relations which prevent the equal satisfaction of basic human needs through innovative products and processes. As an alternative theory, a 'needs-based' argument for inclusive innovation and development has been offered. This argument opens with the non-ideal situation of unequal social relations in innovation and development, and closes with the achievement of equality through socio-technical change brought about by public action and participation. Only principles developed from the bottom up in this way will be able to provide normative guidance towards a more just and innovative global society.

References

Alkire, S. (2002) *Valuing Freedoms: Sen's Capability Approach and Poverty Reduction*, Oxford: Oxford University Press.
Anand, P., Hunter, G., Carter, I., Dowding, K., Guala, F. and van Hees, M. (2007) 'Measurement of Capabilities', *Open Discussion Papers in Economics No.53*, The Open University. Available at: www.oecd.org/site/worldforum06/38363699.pdf [accessed 24 January 2018].
Anand, P. and van Hees, M. (2006) 'Capabilities and Achievements: An Empirical Study', *The Journal of Socio-Economics*, Vol.35, pp. 268–284.
Beitz, C. R. (1986) 'Amartya Sen's Resources, Values and Development', *Economics and Philosophy*, Vol.2, No.2, pp. 282–291.
Beitz, C. R. (2010) 'Justice and International Relations', in G. W. Brown (ed.), *The Cosmopolitan Reader*, Cambridge: Polity Press.
Bentham, J. (1970) 'An Introduction to the Principles of Morals and Legislation', in J. H. Burns and H. L. Hart (eds.), *The Collected Works of Jeremy Bentham*, Oxford: Clarendon Press.
Buchanan, A., Cole, T. and Keohane, R. O. (2011) 'Justice in the Diffusion of Innovation', *The Journal of Political Philosophy*, Vol.19, No.3, pp. 306–332.
Callinicos, A. (2002) 'Marxism and Global Governance', in D. Held and A. McGrew (eds.), *Governing Globalisation*, Cambridge: Polity Press.
Clark, D. A. (2006) 'Capability Approach', in D. A. Clark (ed.), *The Elgar Companion to Development Studies*, Cheltenham: Edward Elgar.
Cohen, G. A. (1989) 'On the Currency of Egalitarian Justice', *Ethics*, Vol.99, pp. 906–944.
Cohen, G. A. (2008) *Rescuing Justice and Equality*, Cambridge, MA and London: Harvard University Press.
Cohen, G. A. and Graham, K. (1990) 'Self-Ownership, Communism and Equality', *Proceedings of the Aristotelian Society*, Vol.64, pp. 25–61.
Cozzens, S. (2007) 'Distributive Justice in Science and Technology Policy', *Science and Public Policy*, Vol.34, No.2, pp. 85–94.
Dunn, J. (1996) *The History of Political Thought and Other Essays*, Cambridge: Cambridge University Press.
Dworkin, R. (1977) *Taking Rights Seriously*, London: Duckworth.
Fleurbaey, M. (2006) 'Capabilities, Functionings and Refined Functionings', *Journal of Human Development*, Vol.7, No.3, pp. 299–310.
Hare, R. M. (1982) 'Ethical Theory and Utilitarianism', in A. Sen and B. Williams (eds.), *Utilitarianism and Beyond*, Cambridge: Cambridge University Press.

Hollis, A. and Pogge, T. (2008) 'The Health Impact Fund: Making New Medicines Accessible for All'. Available at: www.incentivesforglobalhealth.org

Jagger, A. (2006) 'Reasoning about Well-Being: Nussbaum's Methods of Justifying the Capabilities', *Journal of Political Philosophy*, Vol.14, No.3, pp. 109–131.

Kymlicka, W. (1990) *Contemporary Political Philosophy: An Introduction*, Oxford: Oxford University Press.

Lyons, D. (1984) 'Utility and Rights', in J. Waldron (ed.), *Theories of Rights*, Oxford: Oxford University Press.

Mackintosh, M. (1992) 'Introduction', in M. Wuyts, M. Mackintosh and T. Hewitt (eds.), *Development Policy and Public Action*, Oxford: Oxford University Press.

Martell, L. (2011) 'Cosmopolitanism and Global Politics', *The Political Quarterly*, Vol.82, No.4, pp. 618–627.

Médecins San Frontières (2011) *Activity Report 2011*. Available at: www.msf.org/msf/articles/2012/07/international-activity-report-2011.cfm [accessed 24 January 2018].

Mill, J. (1937) *An Essay on Government*, Cambridge: Cambridge University Press.

Nederveen Pieterse, J. (2010) *Development Theory*, London: Sage.

Nozick, R. (1974) *Anarchy, State, and Utopia*, Oxford: Blackwell.

Papaioannou, T. (2011) 'Technological Innovation, Global Justice and Politics of Development', *Progress in Development Studies*, Vol.11, No.4, pp. 321–338.

Papaioannou, T., Yanacopulos, H. and Aksoy, Z. (2009) 'Global Justice: From Theory to Development Action', *Journal of International Development*, Vol.21, pp. 805–818.

Pogge, T. W. (2002) *World Poverty and Human Rights: Cosmopolitan Responsibilities and Reforms*, Cambridge: Polity Press.

Pogge, T. W. (2005) 'Human Rights and Global Health: A Research Programme', *Metaphilosophy*, Vol.36, pp. 182–209.

Prahalad, C. K. (2005) *The Fortune of the Bottom of the Pyramid: Eradicating Poverty through Profits*, Upper Saddle River and New York: Pearson Education/Wharton School Publishing.

Raphael, D. D. (1994) *Moral Philosophy*, Oxford: Oxford University Press.

Rawls, J. (1972) *A Theory of Justice*, Oxford: Oxford University Press.

Rawls, J. (1982) 'Social Utility and Primary Goods', in A. Sen and B. Williams (eds.), *Utilitarianism and Beyond*, Cambridge: Cambridge University Press.

Rawls, J. (1999a) *The Law of Peoples*, Cambridge, MA: Harvard University Press.

Rawls, J. (1999b) 'Social Unity and Primary Goods', in S. Freeman (ed.), *John Rawls: Collected Papers*, Cambridge, MA: Harvard University Press.

Rosenberg, J. (1994) *The Empire of Civil Society*, London: Verso.

Ryan, M. (2009) 'Patent Incentives, Technology Markets, and Public-Private Biomedical Innovation Networks in Brazil', *World Development*, Vol.38, No.8, pp. 1082–1093.

Sen, A. K. (1980) 'Equality of What?', in S. McMurrin (ed.), *Tanner Lectures on Human Values*, Cambridge: Cambridge University Press.

Sen, A. K. (1995) *Inequality Re-Examined*, Oxford: Oxford University Press.

Sen, A. K. (1999) *Development as Freedom*, Oxford: Oxford University Press.

Sen, A. K. (2009) *The Idea of Justice*, London: Penguin.

Singer, P. (2008) 'Famine, Affluence and Morality', in T. Brooks (ed.), *The Global Justice Reader*, Oxford: Blackwell.

Stewart, F. (2001) 'Women and Human Development: The Capabilities Approach by Martha C. Nussbaum', *Journal of International Development*, Vol.13, No.8, pp. 1191–1192.

Stiglitz, J. E., Sen, A. and Fitoussi, J.-P. (2008) *Report by the Commission on the Measurement of Economic Performance and Social Progress*. Available at: http://ec.europa.eu/eurostat/documents/118025/118123/Fitoussi+Commission+report [accessed 24 January 2018].

Westerhaus, M. and Castro, A. (2006) 'How Do Intellectual Property Law and International Trade Agreements Affect Access to Antiretroviarial Therapy?' *PLoS Medicine*, Vol. 3, No. 8, pp.1230–1236.

Wolff, J. (1998) 'Fairness, Respect, and the Egalitarian Ethos', *Philosophy and Public Affairs*, Vol.27, No.2, pp. 97–122.

Wolff, J. (2009) 'Disadvantage, Risk and the Social Determinants of Health', *Public Health Ethics*, Vol.2, No.3, pp. 214–223.

World Trade Organisation (2001) *Declaration on the TRIPS Agreement and Public Health*. Available at: www.wto.org/english/thewto_e/minist_e/min01_e/mindecl_trips_e.htm [accessed 24 January 2018].

3 The question of inclusive innovation for development

So far I have argued that although inclusivity in innovation matters, existing liberal cosmopolitan theories of justice such as liberal egalitarianism, libertarianism, utilitarianism and the capability approach all fail to provide guidance towards equalising the generation and distribution of new technological products and services. I have also shown how this is mainly due to their ideal nature and philosophical constructivism as well as to their lack of relational socio-political foundations. A smarter 'needs-based' approach to inclusive innovation and development is therefore necessary. This approach should be relational and be founded upon non-ideal principles of equity, recognition and participation. It is only this particular set of principles that can guide relational processes of innovation and development towards global justice. In what follows my aim is to elaborate this alternative approach, examining the impact of innovation systems and development on the poor, and pointing towards a non-ideal direction of justice. The argument that I put forward is both normative and empirical. Emerging innovation and development models have been analysed empirically in terms of their similarities with and differences from traditional systems of innovation and development. However, these emerging models are not by definition inclusive and socially just. Rather they need to be evaluated in terms of relational principles which go beyond the distribution of material resources, capabilities and opportunities. The normative direction of emerging models of innovation and development is, in the final analysis, a matter of both morality and politics.

3.1 A needs-based approach to innovation

My approach to inclusive innovation and development draws on Marx (2000) but also on Anderson (1999), Reader (2006), Marion Young (2001) and especially Brock (2009). According to this approach, innovation and development ought to ensure that persons are able to meet their basic needs. As Brock (2009) points out, recent philosophical literature contains two influential accounts about needs. The first is that of Braybrooke (1987) who defines something as a need 'if without its satisfaction one would be unable to carry out basic social roles; those of citizen, parent, householder, and worker' (Brock, 2009: 64). Such roles require a variety of natural and social needs to be satisfied. However, as Brock (ibid.) observes, not all these needs necessarily apply to everyone.

The second account is that of Doyal and Gough (1991), who insist that 'needs are universalizable preconditions that enable non-impaired participation in any form of life' (Brock, 2009: 64). For them, physical health and the mental competence to make choices are two basic needs which translate into other needs including nutritional goods, clean water, adequate housing, appropriate healthcare, a non-hazardous work environment, security in childhood, and physical and economic security. Doyal's and Gough's definition of needs as 'universal' and 'basic' as possible aims to enable political consensus. This is because, as Reader (2006: 338) points out, the needs-based approach:

> proceeds by identifying a set of "basic needs" then designing political systems to meet those needs. The approach is focused on identifying and supplying resources that are universally needed (water, food, houses, equipment, production systems, schools, hospitals, and community infrastructure).

As innovation is a key element in all these resources, designing innovation systems in addition to political systems is crucial to resolving practical problems of needs-based justice.

In both accounts, claims of needs are different from claims of wants. One person, for example, might have 'y' needs to satisfy but he/she might not want 'z'. Another might want 'z' but not have 'y' needs. Satisfying universal basic needs, including the needs of those who are least empowered or least capable of claiming their right to satisfaction, is crucial for the just reproduction of societies. As Soper (2014: 11) has recently stressed:

> Those opposing any universalist essentialism of needs often promote their pluralist approach as a critique of what they see as the undemocratically ethnocentric optic of objective perspectives on human wellbeing. But this, of course, is a critique that is itself dependent for its coherence on acceptance and promotion of precisely the liberal-enlightenment framework of thinking about rights, autonomy, citizenship and social participation that is lacking in many cultural contexts.

Satisfying universal needs matters both morally and politically because it is indispensable for human functioning in societies. In Brock's view (2009: 65):

> If such needs are not met, we are unable to do anything much at all, let alone to lead a recognizably human life. Meeting needs is essential to our ability to function as human agents.

This has been well known since Marx clearly identified the fundamental nature of needs in relation to agency in society. Marx (1975: 327) argued that:

> Man is a species-being, not only because he practically and theoretically makes the species – both his own and those of other things – his objects but also . . . because he looks upon himself as a universal and therefore free being.

Both universality and freedom are related to the ability of persons to exercise agency. To be able to play social roles and to participate equally in different forms of life as a free agent one has to have one's needs satisfied.

Marx's needs-based 'theory of justice' aimed to achieve exactly this by proposing the following principle: distribution in a (just) society ought to be 'from each according to his ability, to each according to his need' (Marx, 2000: 615). Marx confirms that human needs as such are a fundamental component in any account of justice. The question, then, is whether what Marx argues also applies to an account of justice in innovation. How can new technological products and processes be generated and distributed justly and in such a way that they enable people to meet basic needs? According to Brock (2009: 68):

> Enabling is a process that involves a number of different elements depending on where we are in the process. So if x enables y to z, this might involve: (i) giving goods directly to y to accomplish ends of z-kind; (ii) teaching y skills relevant to her accomplishing z; (iii) helping y with opportunities to exercise the skills to accomplish z; and (iv) helping wean y off her dependence on x.

It might be said that technological innovation is crucial within this process of enabling people to meet their basic needs. Specifically, if x enables y to z, then in innovation terms this might involve: (i) transferring technological products and services directly to y to accomplish the ends of z-kind; (ii) teaching y technological and innovation skills relevant to her accomplishing z; (iii) helping y with opportunities to exercise the innovation skills to accomplish z; and (iv) helping wean y off her dependence on x.

Now recall Sen's capabilities approach to justice. One might agree with Brock (ibid.: 69) that indeed 'The ideas of promoting capabilities and of enabling people to meet needs are not far apart. This should come as no surprise; after all, both approaches seek to uncover the aspects of human experience that are necessary for human flourishing'. Brock goes on to demonstrate that Sen's theory and in particular Nussbaum's case for the importance of capabilities are dependent on human needs. This is because they share with Marx the view that humans are sociable beings and have both needs and dignity. From this it follows that if these basic needs are not satisfied then human beings cannot function with dignity as members of society. Of course, as Marx pointed out, human needs are not static but dynamic. Their content changes in relation to technological innovation and development. In his *Economic and Philosophical Manuscripts* of 1844, Marx recognised that 'it is precisely because total production rises that needs, desires and claims also increase in the same manner as production rises' (Marx, 1975: 290). In each and every successive stage of technological and economic development more sophisticated needs are created. Marx was right in his assessment of needs. Indeed, as Juma (2016: 22) confirms:

> Human needs inspire the search for new technological solutions. Conversely, new technologies lead to the emergence of new needs. The simple rules about demand and supply do not apply neatly in dynamic social systems – where new technologies change the character of the economy just as much as the economy leads to the creation of new technological systems.

Certainly, in the 21st century the world is experiencing unprecedented rises in production because of technological innovation. This century is widely recognised among economists and political scientists as the age of plenty in terms of productive forces and capacities. As has already been mentioned, there is both technological and material abundance (Juma, 2013). Advances in science, technology and innovation make it possible for human beings to resolve problems through applications unimaginable by previous generations. Thus, 'The developing world has the potential to access more scientific and technical knowledge than the more advanced countries had in their early stages of industrialisation' (Juma, 2016: 13). As a situation, this serves to make global poverty and injustice even more morally and politically shameful. The normative direction of technological innovation is to enable people to meet their basic needs. Some authors (for example Juma, 2013) have already argued that technological innovation and development is a human right. This is also confirmed by the Universal Declaration of Human Rights (UDHR) that in Article 22 states:

> Everyone, as a member of society, has the right to social security and is entitled to realisation . . . of the economic, social and cultural rights indispensable for his dignity and the free development of his personality.

Indeed, as Juma (2013) points out, this UDHR Article 22 on human development presents a basic needs approach. Article 25 of UDHR declares that:

> Everyone has the right to a standard of living adequate for the health and well-being of himself and his family, including food, clothing, housing and medical care and necessary social services.

This basic needs approach to human rights in general and to technological innovation and development in particular is not surprising. As Brock (2009: 72) argues:

> We must know what our basic needs are before we can sensibly define the entitlements that will be protected by human rights. In order to draw up a list of our human rights we must have a sense of our basic needs.

A needs-based approach to technological innovation has a number of advantages: first, it is not in competition with the human rights approach; second, it is able to appeal to the poor globally; third, it can be crucial for formulating science, technology and innovation policies in connection with development policies.

However, a needs-based approach to technological innovation cannot rely on a top-down politics of liberal cosmopolitanism. As has been argued in the previous chapter, such a politics is undermined by the clashing material interests of powerful global actors. The alternative route emerging is thus that of bottom-up public action and campaigning for just innovation and development, and the meeting of basic needs. In the next chapter, I will discuss in more detail the relationship between public action and non-ideal principles of justice. For the time being, I shall limit myself to analysing the implications of a needs-based approach to innovation for the so-called innovation systems and development.

3.2 Innovation systems and development

A needs-based approach to innovation requires us to revise our understanding of traditional innovation systems and development (Edquist, 1997;

Freeman & Soete, 1997; Lundvall, 1992). Such understanding has traditionally been based on Schumpeter's *Theory of Economic Development* (1983) that recognises the primary role of market-driven and profit-incentivised enterprises in the production of new goods and services. This is what Chataway et al. (2013: 5) regard as 'innovation from above'. This 'innovation from above' co-evolves with unequal institutional arrangements and oppressive organisational structures, failing to incorporate the basic needs, interests and aspirations of the poor. The traditional innovation systems perspective only takes into account the network of organisations, enterprises and individuals focused on generating 'innovation from above' as well as the institutions and policies that affect diffusion of new technological goods and services. This means it is unable to explain the basic needs drive of 'innovation from below'. As Kaplinsky et al. (2009: 186) point out:

> Initially put forward by economists such as Nelson and Freeman in the 1980s to explain the rapid economic growth of the so-called newly industrialising countries (NICs) over the later part of the twentieth century, the use of innovation systems has been extended and developed widely over the past decades.

This wide extension tended to emphasise the quality of 'technology linkages' and 'knowledge flows' among and between well-networked actors in developing countries, missing the rather different institutional context of low-income economies.

In the first decade of the 21st century, Prahalad (2005) came to recognise the importance of that context for 'innovation from below'. The rapid rise in incomes at the 'bottom of the pyramid (BoP)' has facilitated the inclusion of some basic needs in the innovation processes of a number of multinational companies such as Unilever, Nestlé and General Electric. However, these capitalist profit-making enterprises have ignored some other basic needs which cannot be expressed as 'effective demand'. As Srinivas (2014) reminds us, there is a difference between 'need' and 'effective demand'. Some needs, such as, for example, healthcare and renewable energy, may remain unexpressed as effective demand in the market. Effective demand as such is about willingness to pay. Srinivas (ibid.: 5) points out that:

> Innovating organisations and entrepreneurs in principle pursue innovation because of projected demand and not existing needs. But frequently existing needs are mistaken for effective demand.

In this sense, traditional innovation systems have focused on strengthening the institutional framework within which supply of new products and processes address effective demand. These products and processes rarely lead to development. Rather they emerge from formal scientific, techno- logical and productive structures and organisations which confuse or ignore the difference between needs and effective demand. Thus, as Santiago (2014: 1) points out, 'The expected trickle-down redistributive effects and corresponding improvements in prosperity and wealth associated with inno- vation are neither immediate nor automatic'.

In fact, traditional innovation systems are failing the poor in a number of respects: first, the quantity and quality of poverty-relevant innovations are limited; second, potentially poverty-relevant innovations do not scale; and third, some innovations which reach the poor have sub-optimal impacts. Therefore, unless they are radically revised, traditional innovation systems are unable to promote the needs drive of innovation from below. The recent normative turn of innovation studies to equity and, more specifically, to the basic needs approach to inclusivity can provide fundamental understand- ing of new emerging models of 'innovation from below' in terms of their impact on people's lives and capabilities.

3.3 Emerging models of innovation

What do we mean by 'new emerging models of innovation'? What are their characteristics? How inclusive are such models in terms of meeting the basic needs and interests of poor people? By reviewing the growing litera- ture on this topic, one can identify two emerging models of innovation: 'fru- gal' innovations, i.e. simplified versions of existing technological products; and 'grassroots or below the radar' innovations, i.e. innovations generated by low- and middle-income groups drawing on traditional knowledge and available technologies.

Both 'frugal' and 'grassroots or below the radar' innovations can be justi- fied as new models because they embody a number of social and technical changes. Heeks et al. (2014: 2) summarise these changes as follows:

• Significant involvement of the private sector and global value chains in innovation for the poor;
• The development of poor consumers as an accessible mass market;
• Growth and technological capabilities within developing countries; and
• The involvement of new technologies, especially information and com- munication technologies such as mobile phones.

In fact, emerging models of innovation respond to the dominant para- digms of exclusive innovation and have the potential to disrupt global value chains and hierarchies of innovation (Kaplinsky et al., 2009). The most crucial characteristic of emerging models of innovation is that they engage poor people at the BoP as both consumers and producers who actively participate in driving innovation and growth. The incentives of BoP innovators are often reactionary to perceived social injustice in dominant innovation paradigms. Thus, the OECD (2013) stresses that emerging models of innovation for or by low- and middle-income groups are essential for inclusive growth. The question is, how can we be certain that this is the case? In what follows I will attempt an initial evaluation by examining a number of specific cases of frugal and grassroots or below the radar innovations in more detail.

Frugal innovation

The term 'frugal innovation' was introduced in India to describe attempts to cut out the luxury and unnecessary features of high-tech products developed for high-income markets (Chataway et al., 2013). This new model of innovation has been conceptualised as 'innovation for low- and middle-income groups' (OECD, 2013: 30). Given that frugal innovations are often lower-quality versions of more sophisticated technological products and processes, they allow the poor to buy them at affordable prices, meeting some basic needs and increasing welfare benefits. The OECD has listed a number of cases of frugal innovations. However, for the purpose of this chapter, I shall focus on two of them.

Case 1: Computer-Based Functional Literacy (CBFL) in India. This is an innovation inspired by the high percentage of poor people who are illiterate in India. The Tata Group has developed the CBFL technique to teach an illiterate individual to read after only 40 hours of training, at US$2 per individual. The technique is innovative in that it involves animated graphics and a voiceover that explains the relationship between alphabets and the structure and meaning of important everyday words. CBFL has so far helped more than 20,000 poor people learn to read and the ambition is for the technique to become available for agriculture and healthcare teaching.

Case 2: Money Maker Irrigation Pump (MMIP) in Kenya. This innovation was designed by the KickStart International NGO, and has been used by some poor Kenyan farmers at a cost of US$100 per pump. The foot-powered pump costs less than a diesel pump and can irrigate up to two acres of land per day. MMIP has helped a number of poor farmers to move from rain-fed agriculture to irrigated farming, boosting their annual income by US$1000 per farmer and increasing crop diversity. KickStart estimates it has helped lift more than 400,000 people out of poverty.

Both cases are driven by demand for cheap and 'low-tech' products. However, they do not necessarily meet basic education and food needs, as the recent OECD report (2013) implies. The fact that there are differences between lower- and higher-income groups in terms of demand for such frugal innovations is mainly due to price constraints rather than to basic needs. The determining role of cost is also reflected in the cheap modification of products such as mobile handsets and handheld electrocardiograms by northern-based transnational companies (TNCs) such as Nokia and General Electric. The objective of these TNCs is not that of widening access per se, but profit from low-income markets via economies of scale. Indeed, according to OECD (ibid.: 37), the promise is that:

> of accessing new growing markets, such as India and China with their enormous populations. Because even the middle class in such countries has comparatively low incomes, efforts to provide lower-cost alternatives can be attractive.

Given this fact, the argument that demand for frugal innovations reflects basic needs is only partly correct. Some basic needs for quality food and good education can simply not be met by cheap 'low-tech' or modified innovations. As will be argued in the next section, inclusiveness is a multidimensional concept that cannot be realised if people are offered low-quality products. This might explain why in particular developmental contexts some people resist being included as consumers of cheap and low-quality innovations. The example of the Tata Nano car is indicative here. The product was much less successful than predicted, mainly because of quality and safety shortcomings and, as a recent OECD report acknowledges, 'the fact that it was marketed as a "cheap" car which did not appeal to lower-income consumers in search of good-quality products' (OECD, 2015: 21).

Grassroots or below the radar innovation

This is another emerging model of innovation that has been conceptualised by the OECD as 'innovation by low- and middle-income groups' (ibid.: 30). In grassroots innovation or BRI, lower-income groups are not only the target consumers but also the innovative producers. This implies that by drawing on indigenous knowledge and relevant technologies, and by forming powerful networks of activists, practitioners and organisations, lower-income groups are able to introduce innovations that solve practical problems in local communities and meet basic needs (Smith et al, 2012). These innovations might represent incremental changes to existing technological products. However, as has been argued elsewhere (Kaplinsky et al., 2009: 191):

A key feature of BRI is the *collective significance* of these various developments underlying innovation as a process. The likelihood, therefore, is for the development of new products in China and India aimed at these low-income markets. The product-process linkage inherent in many sectors . . . leads to a clustering of production technologies which are similarly reflective of operating conditions in these low-income markets.

Apart from the large value of grassroots or BRI for low-income local communities, such innovations are considered to be potentially disruptive of global innovation hierarchies. This is not due to the introduction of new technologies so much as to the new types of consumers which induce grassroots or BRI. As Kaplinsky et al. also stress (ibid.: 192), the existing innovation leaders:

> are unable to either recognise or exploit these new opportunities. Their trajectories and market antennae inhibit them from fully recognising these new opportunities which are 'below the radar'. Their cost structure – with regard to not just their core component technologies, but also the structure of their value chains – makes it difficult to address these markets, even if they are recognised.

The OECD (2013) and also Smith et al. (2017) have listed a number of cases of grassroots or BRI. However, for current purposes, I have selected the following two.

Case 3: Honey Bee Network (HBN). A number of innovations, including pedal-powered washing machines, groundnut diggers, multi-crop threshers, cotton strippers, pedal-powered water pumps and turmeric/ginger planters, have emerged in communities at the bottom of the pyramid. The HBN, founded by Anil Gupta, is a network of volunteers and grassroots innovators who work together to achieve the following five objectives (SRISTI, 2014: 1). Namely, to:

a   Respect, recognise and reward creative people;
b   Help them add value to their innovations and traditional knowledge – with or without blending these with modern science, technology and other institutional knowledge;
c   Reinforce a conservation ethic so that nature, from which we draw so much, is nourished;
d   Lobby to protect their intellectual property rights, and to generate material and non-material incentives for individuals and communities; and

e   Embed their values, creativity and knowledge systems in the educational system and governance of the society.

The HBN is supported institutionally by the Society for Research and Initiatives for Sustainable Technologies and Institutions (SRISTI). SRISTI was established in 1993 to provide organisational, intellectual and logistics support to the network. According to SRISTI (2014: 2), its primary objectives are to:

a   Systematically document, disseminate and develop green grassroots innovations;
b   Provide intellectual property rights protection to grassroots innovations;
c   Work on the in situ and ex situ conservation of local biodiversity; and
d   Provide venture support to grassroots innovators.

Through SRISTI the HBN has identified and documented hundreds of such grassroots innovations while, in turn, the National Innovation Foundation (NIF) in India has tried to scale them up, applying them to solve similar problems elsewhere. The NIF is an autonomous body of the Indian Department of Science and Technology (DST) that was set up in the year 2000 to (NIF-India, 2013: 2):

•   help India become an innovative and creative society;
•   ensure evolution and diffusion of grassroots green innovations;
•   provide institutional support in scouting, spawning, sustaining and scaling up grassroots green innovations;
•   seek self-reliance through competitive advantage of innovation-based enterprises;
•   build linkages between excellence in formal scientific systems and informal knowledge systems; and
•   promote wider social awareness, and possible applications of the know-how generated as a result of these initiatives in commercial or social spheres.

Different methods of information gathering have been used, including active attempts to look for community-based innovations and traditional knowledge. Walking through Indian villages and holding village meetings is one of these methods. According to SRISTI (2014), once every six months a *Shodh Yatra* organised by volunteers takes place for a period of seven to ten days in selected locations among a cluster of villages. As they go on to explain (ibid.: 17):

> *Shodh Yatra* is a journey in search of knowledge, creativity and innovations at the grassroots [*sic*]. It is an attempt to reach out to the remotest

parts of the country with a firm belief that necessity created from hardships and the challenges of natural surroundings are the prime motivators of creativity and innovations.

The central argument for *Shodh Yatra* has been that poor people have always had to rely on their own ingenuity to solve their problems, far away from high-technology innovation systems which are based on R&D. In so doing, they have developed an alternative grassroots innovation system. What the HBN initiative has done is to identify and document these alternative innovations. Indeed, as Smith et al. (2017) stress:

> The initiative that began in a small way in the state of Gujarat today has the recognition and support of central government for the organisation of a separate mainstream system of innovation to promote grassroots innovations identified by the HBN from across India's states.

Case 4: Social Technologies Network (RTS: Rede de Tecnologia Social) in Brazil. A number of innovations, including portable water storage, biodigesters for home energy, solar dryers or solar desalters, socio-participatory certification and community gardens, for example, have provided solutions that lead to social inclusion and improvement of livelihoods. These innovations are not only characterised by simplicity and low cost but also by their ability to generate income and to improve the quality of life of local communities by leading to development. They are re-applicable in the sense that they can be recreated and appropriated by local populations (Smith et al., 2017). RTS in Brazil used to comprise more than 800 public institutions, social movements and NGOs. It involved groups from across South America in generating and disseminating innovations for development equally. The Brazilian state was also present. This is because the network was 'an explicit attempt to bridge the role of the state and its public policies with the mobilisation of social movements and NGOs' (ibid.: 127). The main goals of this network of public actors and campaigners were democratisation, accessibility and continuous improvement. Local learning and the empowering of communities to innovate to enable them to meet their basic needs were key elements. This process implies a normative and political agenda, one that rejects control and hierarchies in generating innovative products and promoting creativity of producers and consumers. Grassroots or BRI innovation through RTS in Brazil was based on the recognition that the hierarchical technological patterns of the North's neo-liberal profit-seeking innovation – what is often termed 'the Schumpeterian motor' (Chataway et al., 2013) – have so far led to innovation exclusion and poverty. In contrast to this, grassroots or BRI innovation through the RTS promoted inclusiveness that involved local communities and transferred their knowledge and innovations to other populations. These counter-hegemonic technological patterns can generate income and employment from communities, social movements and organisations. However, despite its success, RTS in Brazil was suspended in 2012 due to 'irreconcilable differences between civil society organisations and funders over its formal structure, funding and pace of development' (Smith et al., 2017).

Both cases of grassroots or BRI innovation I have discussed are driven not only by demand for cheap problem-solving products, but also by normative and political principles of equity and participation. Indeed, these innovations are crucial in terms of empowering local communities to meet their basic needs. In India, intellectual inspiration for grassroots innovations can be traced back to the teachings of Mahatma Gandhi and Rabindranath Tagore, both of whom supported a needs-based approach to science, technology and innovation. This is the reason why grassroots innovations are developed and scaled up through local networks, not-for-profit organisations of NGOs and social movements. As Chataway et al. (2013: 22) confirm, such networks and organisations 'remain a considerable source of inclusive innovation today, even though much of this occurs "below the radar" and does not surface in many of the measures used to measure innovation such as patents, R&D, sales and trade'. Grassroots networks often operate in informal social and economic contexts. According to the OECD (2015: 22), 'in 2007, the informal economy amounted to 14% of gross domestic product (GDP) in China, 45.1% in Colombia, 25.6% in India, 20.9% in Indonesia and 31.7% in South Africa'.

Grassroots networks of public actors and social movements for innovation are distinct from traditional movements. They are driven by local initiatives which often challenge social and political structures of marginalisation and exclusion, pushing for change. As Smith et al. (2013: 2) point out:

> Grassroots innovation is an explicitly normative agenda, which seeks to mobilise distinctly political processes, such as claims to social justice, and often questions organisational and economic assumptions in conventional innovation policies. Alternative initiatives tend to arise in civil society and solidarity economy arenas, where groups experiment with social innovations as well as developing 'appropriate technologies' responsive to local situations and needs.

The politics of grassroots innovation is predominately non-cosmopolitan. It moves from the bottom up and is based on local community initiatives rather than following institutional top-down processes and assuming cosmopolitan ideals. Does this imply, therefore, that grassroots innovation initiatives are more likely to meet the requirements of needs-based justice?

The answer is not straightforward. As will be discussed in the next paragraphs, emerging models of innovation are not all necessarily inclusive of the basic needs and aspirations of the poor. They do, however, seem to be better positioned to improve human lives and increase capabilities than traditional models of innovation.

Emerging models of innovation and inclusiveness

As I have pointed out, the OECD (2015, 2013) and a number of researchers (Chataway et al., 2013; Smith et al., 2017; Kaplinsky et al., 2009) tend to regard all new models of innovation for development as inclusive models without providing a normative theory or a clear evaluative framework of innovation inclusiveness. The question that remains unanswered is: how can one understand, evaluate or even measure frugal and grassroots or BRI innovation in terms of inclusiveness? To answer this I shall need to revisit my earlier discussion of the concept of inclusiveness to stress that it is not a politically neutral concept. That is to say, the meaning of inclusive innovation within a liberal politics of justice is different from its meaning within a non-liberal or socialist politics of justice. For liberals, inclusive innovation might be translated as the formal right of each individual to be included in market processes and outcomes. For non-liberals or socialists, however, it might be translated as the substantive and equitable participation of society as a whole in innovation processes and outcomes which are not necessarily market led. Everyone is recognised as being capable of innovating for the satisfying of human needs, rather than simply consuming.

Revisiting my earlier criticism of the liberal cosmopolitan approach to inclusive innovation provides us with a good basis for applying or operationalising the suggestion that the basic needs approach might in fact offer a more plausible framework of evaluation. The argument behind this suggestion is that the basic needs approach offers a non-institutional framework that allows for new models of innovation such as frugal and grassroots or BRI to be evaluated in terms of their contribution towards satisfying natural and social needs. Given that equity, participation and recognition constitute essential criteria of this evaluative framework, the question that arises is to what extent specific cases of frugal innovation (i.e. cases 1 and 2) and specific cases of grassroots or BRI (i.e. cases 3 and 4) satisfy these criteria by meeting equitable needs, improving participation and recognition.

If we begin with cases 1 and 2, existing evidence suggests that neither CBFL nor MMIP are equitable and/or participatory innovations. Both come at a price that, by definition, excludes those who live in poverty, i.e. less than US$1.25 per day. The absolute poor in India and Kenya who are unable to purchase CBFL and/or MMIP are also unable to meet their need to learn reading/writing skills and/or to improve their farming techniques. In cases 1 and 2, by clearly excluding the poorest, frugal innovations promote inequitable inclusiveness of people and places. CBFL and MMIP cannot, therefore, be seen as a means to development for everyone. In addition to this, they are neither participatory innovations nor innovations which lead to recognition of the excluded. There is no evidence to suggest that poor consumers were recognised and involved in the conception and production of CBFL and MMIP. Rather, the Tata Group in India and the KickStart International NGO in Kenya introduced these frugal innovations as rent-seeking enterprises which were better able to understand local markets and use locally available resources. In fact, CBFL and MMIP remain 'innovations from above' (Chataway et al., 2013) which fail to meet any of the basic needs of those on the lowest incomes or the participatory needs of those outside the elite innovatory clique. The same holds true for other frugal innovations such as ultra low-cost mobile handsets, solar energy systems for the poor, low-cost word processing and email devices. (OECD, 2015). None of these innovations are absolutely inclusive of poor consumers and places, neither do they satisfy the relational principles of equity and participation in processes and outcomes.

Moving on to cases 3 and 4, existing evidence suggests that both HBN and RTS may be participatory networks but not necessarily equitable ones. Both networks include innovators such as farmers and entrepreneurs, policymakers, academics and NGOs who are committed to identifying and rewarding innovative ideas and traditional knowledge produced at grassroots level by poor citizens and their communities. Interaction between communities and technology developers leads the latter adopting and benefiting from grassroots or BRI. However, given existing relations of power and domination within the communities and wider socio-political structures of inequality, these benefits are not always equally distributed between poor consumers. In addition, there are high transaction costs to the identification and documentation of grassroots or BRI, and low commercialisation prospects. But, despite problems of equity, grassroots or BRI are more likely to satisfy basic needs than frugal innovations. This is for two reasons: first, grassroots or BRI are less exclusive of the poorest, i.e. those who live on less than US$1.25 per day. The absolute poor in India and Brazil are able to use the HBN and RTS innovations provided they have a connection to these networks. To put it another way, grassroots or BRI promote collective empowerment for the meeting of local needs. Through networks such as HBN and RTS, innovation and development cease to be the privilege of specific individuals and begin to include the whole community. This is the reason why, in a recent article, Smith and Stirling (2018) argue that grassroots or BRI can in fact contribute to innovation democracy. Indeed, grassroots or BRI processes can support citizens' activities by creating empowering socio-technical solutions to problems, meeting needs and contributing to the health of democracy (ibid.).

Certainly, more rigorous investigation and critical insights are necessary in order to show how grassroots or BRI contribute to improving the livelihoods of people and the health of democracy in low-income communities. In addition, questions need to be raised about the possibility of such innovations being scaled up in high-income countries. This is because, as Hernán and Fressoli (2011: 14) stress:

> social exclusion is not circumscribed to under-developed countries; it is merely more apparent and seems crueller there. However, observing the shortcomings of healthcare systems, the social integration problems and the environmental risks that riddle the so-called 'developed' countries, as well as the restriction in access to goods and services, is enough to notice the inability of the market economy to solve key social issues.

In other words, grassroots or BRI might also be able to remedy specific market failures in developed countries, replacing existing innovations which exacerbate social problems.

3.4 Inclusive innovation for development

The fact that emerging models of innovation are not by definition inclusive of people's basic needs, by satisfying normative principles of equity, participation and recognition, raises the question of precisely what inclusive innovation for development requires.

So far I have defended a needs-based approach to innovation that is founded upon these overarching relational principles. By following this approach, my assumption is that innovation systems in the global south (but also in the global north) can become more normative and political in their directions, promoting just and transformative development for all. In other words, they can reconcile economic and social goals, something that no traditional innovation system to date has been able to do. As Foster and Heeks (2013) and Cozzens and Sutz (2012) have stressed, inclusive innovation is not only about the economic output but also about the social process. Many case studies have confirmed that inclusive innovation systems are predominantly local and involve public action and campaigning from poor community members (Smith & Stirling, 2018). Thus, for example, Couto Soares and Cassiolato (2013) show that from the healthcare systems of rural South Africa and the state of Amapá, Brazil (which blend different kinds of knowledge and traditions to produce medicine), to the indigenous health system in the Indian state of Kerala and the Uruguayan public hospitals in poor regions (which drive context-specific technologies), the involvement of local poor communities in innovation is very strong.

Similarly, Smith et al. (2017), in *Grassroots Innovation Movements*, demonstrate the existence of diverse social groups and networks which offer an alternative approach to top-down innovation. This is based on the premise that 'people at grassroots level already have the ideas, knowledge and tools and capabilities required to create their own innovative solutions to climate change and sustainable development' (ibid.: 1). Indeed, contemporary science, technology and innovation institutions have continuously lagged behind in failing to recognise these grassroots modes of knowledge which sometimes compete with the modern R&D-based generation of knowledge in university research centres and firms (ibid.). Although the main purpose of the latter is profit-making in capitalist markets, that of the former is socio-technical change leading towards equalising relations, promoting solidarity, recognising disadvantaged groups and participating in both the production and distribution of innovative solutions to problems of basic needs. Grassroots or BRI are committed to these bottom-up normative frameworks.

Does this mean that the state and political institutions play no particular role in inclusive innovation for development? The answer is in the negative. It is important to stress that such institutions are collective properties which define the values of the innovation game. People innovate within institutions where they internalise the rules and understand that others have expectations about how things are done (Young, 2011). In this sense, the state and political institutions remain important actors for the normative direction of innovation systems. Through public funding for inclusive innovation pathways and procurement of inclusive technologies, the state can substantially encourage needs-based justice in this area. However, this does not change the fact that public action and campaigning are key to new inclusive innovation initiatives in local contexts. The state in low- and middle-income developing countries may not be a risk-taker in the sense that economists such as Lazonick and Mazzucato (2013) define the term (i.e. be an entrepreneurial state) for high-income developed countries, but it certainly has the administrative power to co-ordinate the different sets of institutions and organisations which are crucial for inclusion. As Couto Soares and Cassiolato (2013: 13) point out: 'Such organisations, including research institutions and government enterprises with different specialisations and hospitals, interact and collaborate with one another and benefit from their specific type of knowledge base'.

Concluding remarks

A smarter 'needs-based' approach to inclusive innovation appears to be one that can be founded upon non-ideal principles of equity, recognition and participation. This is because it is a bottom-up approach that derives its normativity from public action and campaigning for inclusive innovation. Emerging models at BoP, whether frugal or grassroots, need to be analysed as examples of this bottom-up approach. However, it would be a mistake to brand uncritically all frugal and/or grassroots innovations as being by definition inclusive. These emerging models must first be evaluated in terms of a clear framework that can ensure they meet the minimum requirements of justice. Clearly, such requirements must go beyond the distribution of resources, capabilities and opportunities to include the equalisation of relations in innovation.

References

Anderson, E. S. (1999) 'What Is the Point of Equality?', *Ethics*, Vol.109, No.2, pp. 287–337.

Braybrooke, D. (1987) *Meeting Needs*, Princeton, NJ: Princeton University Press.

Brock, G. (2009) *Global Justice: A Cosmopolitan Account*, Oxford: Oxford University Press.

Chataway, J., Hanlin, R. and Kaplinsky, R. (2013) 'Inclusive Innovation: An Architecture for Policy Development', *IKD Working Paper No.65*, The Open University. Available at: www.open.ac.uk/ikd/documents/working-papers/ikd-working-paper-65.pdf [accessed 26 January 2018].

Couto Soares, M. C. and Cassiolato, J. E. (2013) 'Innovation Systems and Inclusive Development: Some Evidence Based on Empirical Work', paper submitted to the International Workshop on *New Models of Innovation for Development*, Manchester University.

Cozzens, S. and Sutz, J. (2012) *Innovation in Informal Settings: A Research Agenda*, Ottawa: IDRC.

Doyal, L. and Gough, I. (1991) *A Theory of Human Needs*, Basingstoke: Palgrave Macmillan.

Edquist, C. (1997) *Systems of Innovation: Technologies, Institutions and Organisations*, London: Pinter.

Foster, C. and Heeks, R. (2013) 'Conceptualising Inclusive Innovation: Modifying Systems of Innovation Framework to Understand Diffusion of New Technology to Low-Income Consumers', *European Journal of Development Research*, Vol.25, No.3, pp. 333–355.

Freeman, C. and Soete, L. (1997) *The Economics of Industrial Innovation*, 3rd ed., London and New York: Routledge.

Heeks, R., Foster, C. and Nugroho, Y. (2014) 'New Models of Inclusive Innovation for Development', *Innovation and Development*, Vol.4, No.2, pp. 175–185.

Hernán, T. and Fressoli, M. (2011) 'Technologies for Social Inclusion in Latin America: Analysing Opportunities and Constraints; Problems and Solutions in Argentina and Brazil'. Available at: https://smartech.gatech.edu/bitstream/handle/1853/42606/657-1817-2-PB.pdf [accessed 26 January 2018].

Juma, C. (2013) 'Technological Innovation and Human Rights: An Evolutionary Approach', *Working Paper*, Harvard Kennedy School.

Juma, C. (2016) *Innovation and Its Enemies: Why People Resist New Technologies*, Oxford: Oxford University Press.

Kaplinsky, R., Chataway, J., Clark, N., Hanlin, R., Kale, D., Muraguri, L., Papaioannou, T., Robbins, P. and Wamae, W. (2009) 'Below the Radar: What Does Innovation in Emerging Economies Have to Offer Other Low-Income Economies?', *International Journal of Technology Management & Sustainable Development*, Vol.8, No.3, pp. 177–197.

Lazonick, W. and Mazzucato, M. (2013) 'The Risk-Reward Nexus in the Innovation-Inequality Relationship: Who Takes the Risks? Who Gets the Rewards?', *Industrial and Corporate Change*, Vol.22, No.4, pp. 1093–1128.

Lundvall, B.-A. (1992) *National Systems of Innovation: Towards a Theory of Innovation and Interactive Learning*, London: Pinter.

Marx, K. (1975) *Early Writings*, London: Penguin.

Marx, K. (2000) 'The Communist Manifesto', in D. McLellan (ed.), *Karl Marx: Selected Writings*, Oxford: Oxford University Press.

NIF (2013) *National Innovation Foundation-India*, Ahmedabad: NIF.

OECD (2013) *Innovation and Inclusive Development*, Conference Discussion Report revised, February 2013. Available at: www.oecd.org/sti/inno/oecd-inclusive-innovation.pdf [accessed 24 January 2018].

OECD (2015) *Innovation Policies for Inclusive Development: Scaling Up Inclusive Innovations*. Available at: www.oecd.org/innovation/inno/scaling-up-inclusive-innovations.pdf [accessed 26 January 2018].

Prahalad, C. K. (2005) *The Fortune of the Bottom of the Pyramid: Eradicating Poverty through Profits*, Upper Saddle River and New York: Pearson Education/Wharton School Publishing.

Reader, S. (2006) 'Does a Basic Needs Approach Need Capabilities?', *The Journal of Political Philosophy*, Vol.14, No.3, pp. 337–350.

Santiago, F. (2014) 'Innovation for Inclusive Development', *Innovation and Development*, Vol.4, No.1, pp. 1–4.

Schumpeter, J. A. (1983) *The Theory of Economic Development*, New Brunswick and London: Transaction Publishers.

Smith, A., Arond, E., Fressoli, M., Hernán, T. and Abrol, D. (2012) 'Supporting Grassroots Innovation: Facts and Figures', *SciDev*. Available at: www.scidev.net/en/science-and-innovation-policy/supporting-grassroots-innovation/features/supporting-grassroots-innovation-facts-and-figures-1.html [accessed 26 January 2018].

Smith, A., Fressoli, M., Abrol, D., Arond, E. and Ely, A. (2017) *Grassroots Innovation Movements*, London and New York: Routledge.

Smith, A., Fressoli, M. and Hernán, T. (2013) 'Grassroots Innovation Movements: Challenges and Contributions', *Journal of Cleaner Production*. Available at:

www.sciencedirect.com/science/article/pii/S0959652612006786 [accessed 26 January 2018].

Smith, A. and Stirling, A. (2018) 'Innovation, Sustainability and Democracy: An Analysis of Grassroots Contributions', *Journal of Self-Governance and Management Economics*, Vol.6, No.1, pp. 64–97.

Soper, K. (2014) 'On Human Needs', *The Centre for the Study of Democracy Bulletin*, Vol.19, Nos.1–2, pp. 11–13.

Srinivas, S. (2014) 'Demand and Innovation: Paths to Inclusive Development', in S. V. Ramani (ed.), *Innovation in India: Combining Economic Growth with Inclusive Development*, Cambridge: Cambridge University Press.

SRISTI (2014) *A Voice for Grassroots Innovators*, Ahmedabad: SRISTI.

Young, I. M. (2001) 'Activist Challenges to Deliberative Democracy', *Political Theory*, Vol.29, pp. 670–690.

Young, I. M. (2011) *Responsibility for Justice*, Oxford: Oxford University Press.

4 Generating non-ideal principles of justice through public action

So far I have defended and elaborated a needs-based approach to inclusive innovation and development. According to this approach, in order for novel technological products and processes to be inclusive, the basic needs and aspirations of the poor must be incorporated in knowledge generation and innovative production. The extent to which such incorporation will be socially just depends on the application of bottom-up principles of equity, recognition and participation in relations of innovative production and distribution. Given that none of these principles can be constructed as ideal principles, the question that arises is how they can be generated to ensure that their normativity is effective. This chapter explores the way in which, through public action and campaigning, the generation of non-ideal principles becomes possible. The normative framework within which innovation and development are able to be socially just is founded upon bottom-up political processes. Such processes may be different from country to country. However, what remains universal about them is that they are able to promote cosmopolitan justice in innovation and development through non-cosmopolitan campaigns and local activism. In what follows, I discuss the nature of non-ideal principles, the role of public action and the bottom-up political process through which equity, recognition and participation can be justified as normative principles of inclusive innovation.

4.1 The nature of non-ideal principles

Non-ideal principles can be thought of as principles which cannot guide a perfectly just society, but which can help us deal with current injustices and move towards something better (Anderson, 2010) in terms of social relations in innovation. According to Ypi (2012: 38) such principles are 'able to guide agency in empirically contingent circumstances'. Agency plays a crucial role in the identification, interpretation and articulation of non-ideal principles. This implies a pragmatic approach to social justice in innovation. Non-ideal theory is not a derivative of ideal theory. We do not first need to know what constitutes an ideally just society in order to identify where exactly our society falls short. Rather, we need to begin by exploring the existing problems and complaints of that society before we can hope to have any idea of what would be most just (Anderson, 2010). An abstract model of an ideal world of justice in innovation cannot provide credible suggestions about what ought to be done. An empirical account of our non-ideal world, however, can provide the ground for engaging in a non-ideal interpretation and subsequent theorising.

Clearly, this particular way of theorising is in contradistinction to the liberal egalitarian, the libertarian and the utilitarian approaches to justice. In particular Rawls, Nozick and Dworkin, but also Pogge and Beitz, start their political philosophies from ideal theory, deriving impartial and universal principles of justice through epistemological assumptions and theoretical constructions such as the 'original position' (Rawls, 1972). Next, political scientists and public policy experts use these principles to identify where exactly our basic social structures and activities, including knowledge generation and innovation structures, fall short in order to fix them through vertical or horizontal policy schemes and interventionary measures. Instead, however, as Anderson (2010: 3) points out:

> There are three basic reasons to start political philosophy from non-ideal theory – from a diagnosis of injustices in our actual world rather than from a picture of an ideal world. First, we need to tailor our principles to the motivational and cognitive capacities of human beings. . . . Second, we risk leaping to the conclusion that any gaps we see between our ideal and reality must be the cause of the problems in our actual world, and that the solution must therefore be to adopt policies aimed at directly closing the gaps. . . . Third, starting from ideal theory may prevent us from recognising injustices in our non-ideal world.

These three reasons justify closer collaboration between political philosophy and empirical social science disciplines such as science, technology, innovation and development studies (Hertzberg, 2014). The focus is no longer on social justice as a political ideal of equal distribution of goods, but as a political issue of equal relations between and within different groups in society, including innovators, users, policymakers and regulators. If one group has control over an important knowledge, skill and/or innovative product such as, for example, essential medicine, and excludes out groups from using it then this is, according to Anderson (2010: 7), a 'group or categorical' inequality that is unjust and needs to be resolved through policy guided by non-ideal principles. As she points out, the spread of categorical inequality comes with the tendency of people to explain and legitimate it by inventing stories about fundamental differences between groups. This is also the case with groups of developed countries such as the US and those of the EU, the pharmaceutical companies of which have acquired dominance in innovative technologies such as genomics and biotechnology, in the process growing bigger and stronger than their counterparts in developing countries. As Piketty (2014) demonstrates, in the end this domination is translated into unequal ownership of capital. The major developed countries and their multinationals own part of the capital of developing countries. But according to Piketty (ibid.: 70–71), 'Inequality of capital ownership is already difficult to accept and peacefully maintain within a single community. Internationally it is almost impossible to sustain without a canonical type of political domination'. Piketty clearly suggests that the equalising of both technological knowledge and innovation diffusion should be the principle mechanism of global and local convergence. In his words: 'The poor catch up with the rich to the extent that they achieve the same level of technological know-how, skill and education, not by becoming the property of the wealthy'.

In fact, injustice and inequality, both global and local, are always relational. They involve oppressive social relationships through which people exercise power, dominate, exploit and marginalise others (Anderson, 1999: 313). Such relationships emerge in different realms, including those of the generation of new knowledge, the production of novel goods and/or services, and the diffusion of innovation to societies. The hierarchical division of labour within capitalism and the unequal distribution of resources through the free market lead to asymmetries of power in these realms. Resolving the problems of injustice and inequality means developing 'a social order in which persons stand in relations of equality' (Anderson, ibid.) in whatever they do, including production and consumption of innovative knowledge, and innovative goods and services. This, in turn, requires us to experiment with different public policies and actions so that evaluative judgements about justice in innovation are focused on relations and are evidence based. Anderson (2014: 379) stresses that:

> Normative judgements may be used to guide either conduct or feeling. If they guide conduct, they are practical; if they guide feeling alone, they are purely evaluative. Most philosophers test purely evaluative judgements in thought experiments: we can imagine the state that is judged to be good, and consider whether we intuitively like or approve of it. However, from a pragmatist's point of view, the ultimate evidence for evaluative judgements lies in actual experiments: how would we feel about the state if we actually experienced it?

Reconstructing Dewey's pragmatism, Anderson explains the nature of non-ideal theory in terms of a trial-error process. This process is political because it involves public action and campaigning to both generate principles and resolve the problem of current injustice. Some of these principles might be tested in developmental contexts and others in developed contexts. The application of non-ideal principles of justice is neither impartial nor universal. Rather it depends on specific problems on the ground. Current injustices in innovation take different forms. From lack of user participation in the generation of innovation to unjustified exclusion of local firms from hierarchical value chains dominated by big corporations and multinationals, injustices in innovation can be dealt with through bottom-up principled solutions. Learning different practices of generating and implementing normative frameworks of justice is of key importance here.

However, non-ideal theory is not uncontested. One criticism has been that it is difficult to separate such theory from ideal approaches to justice simply because contemporary political theorists tend to display features of both (Ypi, 2012). Following from this, Ypi (ibid.) argues that a clear division between the tasks of ideal and non-ideal theory may be unnecessary because an alternative exists that combines both. This alternative is the pursuing of normative theory in an activist mode that Ypi calls 'dialectical' as it emphasises the development of relationship between principles and agency. According to Ypi (ibid.: 41):

> The circumstances of particular conflicts and the analysis of existing social practices lead theorists and other agents occupying relevant social roles to reflect on them and to articulate specific interpretations of the concerns and commitments they express. After various stages of revision and having obtained some basic level of plausibility, these interpretations are combined with certain first-order values and give rise to fundamentally appropriate theories, theories that are in turn invoked to guide political action.

It might be argued that the main shortcoming of Ypi's argument is her implicit acceptance of the ideal theory's claim that first-order values cannot directly emerge from public action and campaigning. Rather, she implies, they remain privileged products of some kind of 'pure' thought that can then be combined with articulated interpretations of empirical concerns about social and political issues, including innovation. This claim is problematic because it ignores the possibility of normative principles being directly generated from agency. In fact, what Ypi calls 'avant-garde political agents' (in other words, those agents selecting appropriate interpretations of specific political practices) can be thought of as the key generators of normativity through public action and campaigning for social justice. In the case of innovation, the avant-garde agents are almost all engaging in public action, contesting for increased inclusivity in the process of production of novel technological goods and services, to lead to more equitable, participatory and recognised social relations.

4.2   The role of public action in generating normative theory

Public action for inclusive innovation emerges when, for example, unequal access to new technologies and innovative products causes people to fail in satisfying their basic needs (with disturbing consequences for their lives), or when certain innovation hierarchies and top-down value chains fail to respect and recognise different people as both producers and users of innovation. When people understand that the reason they cannot acquire new innovative drugs and therapies for improving their health is that the IPR rules and global hierarchies of innovation have been developed without their democratic participation, or have been captured by groups of rich countries in the global north, they begin to feel politically responsible for the innovation injustice and therefore act intuitively, generating new normative principles and bottom-up solutions to rectify it. In Young's theory, political responsibility is a forward-looking concept that refers to the obligation of a person to join with others who share that responsibility to transform the structural processes to make their outcomes less unjust (Young, 2011).

Young (2001: 672–673) provides us with the general profile of a typical public activist:

> The activist is committed to social justice and normative value and the idea that politically responsible persons ought to take positive action to promote these. He also believes that the normal workings of the social, economic, and political institutions in which he dwells enact or reproduce deep wrongs – some laws or policies have unjust effects, or social and economic structures cause injustice, or non-human animals and things are wrongly endangered, and so on. Since the ordinary rules and practices of these institutions tend to perpetuate these wrongs, we cannot redress them within those rules. The activist opposes particular actions or policies of public or private institutions, as well as systems of policies or actions, and wants them changed. . . . Besides being motivated by a passion for justice, the activist is often also propelled by anger or frustration at what he judges to be the intransigence of people in power in existing institutions who behave with arrogance and indifference toward the injustices the activist finds they perpetuate.

Young (1990) clearly began *Justice and the Politics of Difference* by asking what the implications of various public actions and movements might be for political theories of justice. Although her analysis was focused on feminist, Black liberation, and gay and lesbian movements, in the case of innovation, anger or frustration at top-down innovation systems and hierarchical value chains which disrespect, misrecognise and eventually exclude the needs and aspirations of the poor has increased the pressure for structural changes and transformations that can enable bottom-up or grassroots remedies to innovation injustices. In addition, scarcity and specific problem-solving needs on the ground have induced more inclusive models of grassroots innovation in developing countries. Indeed, as Anderson (2014: 380) argues, 'All great ideals of justice require enduring struggle even in the face of repeated disappointment. The struggles for democracy and free labour have taken hundreds of years and are still continuing'. The same holds true for equality in innovations which satisfy basic needs such as health, food and energy. As Smith et al. (2017) show, public action and campaigning through movements, including grassroots innovation movements, draw on normative framing that involves a critique of top-down, hierarchical and unequal science, technology and innovation. This critique leads to bottom-up interpretations of just and inclusive relations of innovation. Articulating the theories and principles for such social relations very much depends on those activists who reflect on and theorise the bottom-up interpretations of justice and inclusiveness. Activists find themselves in the position of carrying out the non-ideal theorising of inclusive innovation while also playing an active part in it.

Activists' responses to unjust innovative technologies should not be confused with the responses of those whom Juma (2016) criticises as being enemies of innovation, which are based on incorrect public perceptions about the risks and benefits of new technologies together with fear of change. The responses of the latter (ibid.: 24; italics added):

> are often reinforced by social norms of disgust that have evolved among people as self-protection from contact with potential sources of pathogens. This behaviour readily extends to new technologies such as new foods that may be seen as potentially threatening to human health. Or it may be extended to the moral level to protect society in general. Society may also automatically question new technologies on the basis of their essential attributes, which are considered wholesome. In other cases, new technologies may elicit negative responses because they appear to challenge the perceptive view of the natural world or the intentionality of parts of it. Arguments against *playing God* fall in this latter category.

By contrast, the responses of public activists and campaigners for justice in innovation are often reinforced by their sense of political responsibility and of social norms of fairness that have evolved among people as a self-reaction or resistance to hierarchical and oppressive social relations of innovation which tend to threaten their survival. Arguments for equal access to innovative technologies fall into this category. Public activists and campaigners for justice in innovation try to make explicit that innovation is inherently political. Indeed, as Smith and Stirling (2018: 65–66) stress:

> Too often, the very real politics of innovation is masked by technocratic and exclusive approaches imposing narrow criteria of efficiency, profit and convenience. The dominant image (and practice) of innovation continues to focus upon rent-seeking, technology-based firms working with research institutes and investors, aided by a policy environment that facilitates systemic interaction between these institutions in the pursuit of economic growth. Overlooked are the ways these arrangements privilege certain values, interests and positions towards innovation in society, and carry with them a less democratic politics than might be merited by the stakes at hand.

Public activists and campaigners are fully aware of the political fact that innovations shape people's lives and impact on social institutions in profound and pervasive ways (ibid.). By responding to injustice, they try to equalise and democratise social and institutional frameworks. Indeed, there are several cases of public action and campaigning, especially when it comes to high-tech innovations.

Take, for example, the case of public action and campaigning for access to antiretroviral (ARV) drugs in South Africa. In 1996 medical researchers found that a combination of three such drugs could control HIV/AIDS. However, these innovative medicines were patented with the result that their cost would exceed US$10,000 per patient. Such a cost was unaffordable for, and therefore exclusive of, developing countries and, as a result, in 1997 South Africa introduced the Medicines Act to allow the compulsory licensing or parallel importation of ARVs. In response, 39 multinational pharmaceutical companies represented by the Pharmaceutical Manufacturers Association of South Africa (PMA) filed a lawsuit against the South African government, insisting that the Medicines Act breached the TRIPS agreement. Both the US and the EU also increased pressure on South Africa, effectively acting in favour of the big pharmaceutical companies and against the poor. Public activists and campaigners, however, motivated by a commitment to fairness as well as by anger and frustration, mobilised global public opinion against the lawsuit and succeeded in turning it into a major public relations disaster for the pharmaceutical companies (Timmerman, 2013). The argument of the activists was loud and powerful: big pharmaceutical companies violate the human right to health by putting treatments out of financial reach (Wolff, 2012). This argument and the resulting public pressure led to withdrawal of the lawsuit. To put it another way, recognition of the right to health provided the moral justification for equal access to treatments and drugs for HIV/AIDS. This justification then used by activists and campaigners to undermine the legality of the lawsuit. Taking the human right to health seriously necessitates ensuring that there is equal access to health innovation.

Another example of public action and campaigning took place in 1996 on behalf of people living with HIV in Brazil. Seeking to articulate the universal right of access to ARVs, this public action and campaigning led to compulsory licensing provisions which had an impact on the country's pharmaceutical innovation. Indeed, as Wolff (2012: 80) points out, 'Human rights cases, backed by wide, active, popular advocacy, together with media backing, can create an unstoppable force'. In the 21st century, public activists' claims for justice in innovation appear to be gathering momentum. For example, the 2002 global campaign to change South African pharmaceutical legislation so that the antiretroviral (ARV) nevirapine could be made available for public health also tackled broader structural conditions for justice in innovation such as IPRs. The resulting regulatory and policy changes in South Africa had a tremendous impact on the production of new affordable medicines.

Further evidence, including their advocating and lobbying for medical innovation prizes and alternative incentive systems, indicates that global public action organisations such as Health Action International (HAI) and Knowledge Ecology International (KEI) have now moved towards intervening directly in the just production of new knowledge that leads to inclusive innovation (HAI, 2012; KEI, 2009). In addition, other public action organisations and campaigners such as Médecins San Frontières (MSF) have induced just innovations in developmental contexts for poverty-related diseases such as sleeping sickness, malaria and AIDS. These innovations include: diagnosing uncomplicated malaria using a rapid test rather than a microscope; developing the fixed-dose combinations that MSF now uses for treating AIDS and malaria; and participating in malaria treatment trials in refugee camps (MSF, 2011).

Certainly, health innovation is not the only high-tech area in which public action and campaigning have led to positive changes in terms of justice. Software is another important area of activism and campaigning for justice in innovation. Specifically, the limits and shortcomings of the IPR regime that emerged in the neo-liberal era of the 1980s led to important public actions and campaigns which aimed to restore free and open access to software development by creating 'knowledge commons'. Consider, for example, the case of the F/LOSS (Free/Libre and Open Source Software) movement. According to Coriat (2015: 13):

> there is no doubt that what has been done under the aegis of the F/LOSS (Free/Libre and Open Source Software) movement was the first successful tentative at a very large scale to introduce new nodes of production of innovation. As such F/LOSS can be considered as a locus of the archetypical 'knowledge commons'.

Indeed, the F/LOSS movement was a response to the extension of IPRs (mainly copyrights and patents) to mathematical algorithms that enabled software to be sold as a commodity. Previously software had been produced in a co-operative way by developers sharing their skills. The F/LOSS movement began when software developers decided to produce their own tools, generating new principles of openness, co-operation, participation and recognition to guide their activities. To do so, they had to protect their inventions from privatisation and ensure they could remain in the public domain. Thus, as Coriat (ibid.: 14) points out:

> through the F/LOSS foundation emerged a series of legal innovations. Among them a key institutional innovation was the GNU GPL license that guarantees the cumulativeness of progress through free access to innovation.

The main incentive of software developers to join this particular public action and campaign for a 'knowledge commons' was to benefit from the creativity of other participants and to be recognised for their own skills of innovation. Another incentive was the lack of hierarchy and power domination among the community developers. The F/LOSS movement, like many others, appears to be a knowledge producer, drawing ideas from different sources to address injustice through innovation. This is not surprising. As Smith et al. (2017: 17) point out:

> social movements act as laboratories of experimentation for new ideas, forms of organisation and knowledge. In this way, social movements and campaigns can be regarded as reflexive social actors in two forms. First, social movements and campaigns are social actors that learn by doing, particularly through reflection and debate concerning experience with movement practices, strategies and forms of organisation (and modified accordingly). Second, social movements produce knowledge

that 'might be inconvenient to and resisted from above' and bring it to the public.

In order to achieve their objectives, social movements and other public actors do not seek exclusive IPRs as an incentive for innovation. Rather, they try to keep these regulatory mechanisms of knowledge privatisation out of their innovative activities. However, this is not to say there are no exceptions to this rule. For example, in India the HBN in general and Anil Gupta in particular chose to endorse strong IPRs as a way of recognising the rights of farmers and grassroots innovators. Thus they proposed to support a notion of cognitive justice through IPRs. 'He [Gupta] suggested that the Indian government should accept the principle that innovators wherever and whoever they might be must be protected and compensated through the institution of strong IPRs' (Smith et al., 2017: 151).

It might be argued that public action and campaigning are not only a force to defend against exclusion from innovative products and processes of vital importance for the poor, but also a force for generating normative principles of justice in innovation. Although the advocacy activities of both high-tech movements such as F/LOSS and low-tech grassroots innovation campaigns such as HBN take place at different levels, contexts and historical times, all such activities are reflexive. As such they are crucial in encouraging people to think critically about top-down ideals which fail to guide equal social relations in innovation, and for proposing new bottom-up principles which can achieve social relations of equity, recognition and participation. This is because, as Young (2001: 676) points out, 'activists are often more self-conscious than political actors about having good reasons for what they do and for disciplining their fellows to follow the rules in their collective actions'. These reasons often go beyond the distributive aspects of justice and towards aspects of recognition and participation; as Young (1990: 1) makes clear, 'distributional issues are crucial to a satisfactory conclusion of justice, [but] it is a mistake to reduce social justice to distribution'.

Indeed, injustice is not limited to the fact that in capitalist societies some people get more than others but also about the lack of recognition of group difference and the right to democratic participation in certain socio-economic and political processes. Young, Fraser and other contemporary theorists of justice clearly demonstrate that equitable distribution, recognition and democratic participation constitute the foundations of justice. This also applies to innovation processes that are, by definition, social, economic and political. A lack of recognition and declining participation in the innovation processes of society lead to a lack of respect for different human needs and to a lack of democracy. New social products and/or services fail to address such needs and therefore innovation becomes the privilege of those who eventually succeed in preventing the normative direction of innovation systems towards inclusion and justice.

4.3 Justifying equity, participation and recognition as bottom-up principles of inclusive innovation

Activists' main argument for inclusive innovation is both moral and political. People ought to be recognised as social actors with rights who participate in equal relations of innovation in society. To put it another way, throughout the interpretations and theorisations of activists and campaigners, equity, recognition and participation seem to emerge as contextualisable bottom-up principles of inclusive innovation. These three principles can be broadly formulated as follows:

> *Equity*: all persons are of equal moral worth and deserve to stand in relations of equality to one another in the processes of innovation generation and distribution.
>
> *Recognition*: all persons ought to be recognised and respected as equals in terms of their basic needs for innovation.
>
> *Participation*: all persons are entitled to equal rights of participation in the innovation process of their societies.

These three principles are just because everyone who follows them in his/her particular innovation and development context has an effective voice in their consideration and is able to agree to them without coercion. For innovation to be inclusive, it must follow these principles enabling all to meet their needs. In this sense, inclusive innovation principles ought to be egalitarian, thus preventing people from entering into superior-inferior relations in the social process of innovation. Faces of oppression, whether they be marginalisation, hierarchy, domination, exploitation or cultural imperialism (Young, 1990), have no place in innovative communities of equals. Such communities are democratic communities in the sense that innovators, regulators and users are not in relations of hierarchy with one another but in relations of equality. Relations of equality as such ought not to be influenced by naturally acquired talents and asymmetries of knowledge, material resources, opportunities and capabilities. Rather, they ought to be based on social co-operation and the sharing of ideas and resources. If the innovation process of a society were wholly just, the principles of equity, recognition and participation would be reflected in every relation between every innovator, regulator and user. As a result, no innovative product and/or process would be exclusive of the interests and aspirations of low-income people.

The three principles of inclusive innovation outlined previously are distinct and cannot be thought of as simply generic elements of the ideal of justice. Rather they should be thought of as concrete principles which have been articulated in various forms through the justice struggles of public activists and campaigners, including civil society organisations, NGOs, social movements and advocacy groups. Specifically, the struggles for equal access to innovative drugs for diseases such as HIV/AIDS, the demands for recognition of the rights of different groups of patients (such as those suffering from neglected diseases) and for democratic participation in the innovation process (so that the basic needs of people in poor communities are addressed through the innovation process) all demonstrate the relational and contextualisable character of bottom-up principles of inclusive innovation. These principles frame public action and campaigning for inclusive innovation as grassroots movements for social justice. According to Smith et al. (2017: 166):

Frames are seen as a fundamental part of the affirmation of collective identity, values, motivations and visions of change, and a reference point for action, as well as being shaped through action. Framing is understood to be a process negotiated among activists, in which commitments towards the promotion of grassroots innovation are given more specific form. Such negotiations seek to prioritise different roles for grassroots factors; suggest different roles for grassroots groups; guide activity towards different opportunities and possibilities in a society; emphasise different kinds of knowledge production and parts of innovation processes or expected outcomes; identify and promote certain exemplary artefacts and technologies; and manifest in contrasting strategies for promoting grassroots innovation.

Pragmatically speaking, public activists and campaigners for inclusive innovation call for better interaction between formal and informal actors and institutions and focus on localised needs and the equal diffusion of frugal and/or grassroots innovations within communities (Papaioannou, 2014; Foster & Heeks, 2013; Smith et al., 2010; Thomas et al., 2012). In addition, as Smith et al. (2017: 52) observe:

activists' practical confrontation with social and economic issues generated a rich plurality of knowledge. Whether highlighting and addressing the exclusions and inequities in existing grassroots innovation . . . or pointing to injustices in society, a figuring-out of issues through material projects proved both informative and expressive for participants. Movement initiatives and spaces permitted finer-grained and more richly textured forms of knowledge production as compared to, say, more rarefied analysis and argument in manifestos, reports and policy documents.

Activists' demands for radical social and institutional changes increasingly undermine traditional and hierarchical innovation systems. In so doing, they pave the way for a normative direction that is more transformative of people's lives and more consistent with the demands of justice. This direction does not only mean opening up innovation to those who, up till now, have been excluded from use of the high- and low-tech products and processes that are crucial for their survival, but also constructing an entirely new set of social relations among the actors involved in the generation and diffusion of new technologies. Such relations, guided by the principles of equity, participation and recognition, go far beyond simplistic 'triple helix' models of innovation that narrowly focus on the main actors such as managers, scholars and public servants (Etzkowitz & Leydesdorff, 1995, 2000). Rather, social relations of innovation are complex and involve multiple actors within political and institutional frameworks and settings, including those of property rights.

In fact, by acting together, it is politics and the state that are able to reinforce an institutional framework within which people can come together in relations of equality to innovate for meeting their basic needs. This argument does not imply the insignificance of the markets as institutions. Rather it implies the political nature of innovative activity within certain market processes of demand. By referring to politics only in passing, traditional innovation studies fail to understand its role in the process of radical or incremental technical change. Even recently, celebrated economists such as Mazzucato (2014) and Perez (2013) who consider the state to be an important political institution for innovation do not seem to provide in-depth understanding of the politics of innovation, let alone explain the role of the state in emerging innovation models in developing countries. Specifically, Mazzucato (2011, 2014) builds on both neo-Schumpeterian and neo-Keynesian arguments, particularly those of Block and Keller (2011), to challenge the liberal and libertarian minimalist views of the state and politics in technological innovation. According to the early version of her argument (published as a report for DEMOS, 2011: 16–17):

the role of the government, in the most successful economies, has gone way beyond creating the right infrastructure and setting the rules. It is a leading agent in achieving the type of innovative breakthroughs that allow companies, and economies, to grow, not just by creating the 'conditions' that enable innovation. Rather the state can proactively create strategy around a new high growth area before the potential is understood by the business community (from the internet to nanotechnology), funding the most uncertain phase of the research that the private sector is too risk-averse to engage with, seeking and commissioning further developments, and often even overseeing the commercialisation process. In this sense it has played an important entrepreneurial role.

Certainly, Mazzucato's argument is not founded upon a political theory of the state. In fact, it is not clear at all whether her understanding of the state is, for example, Weberian, liberal, pluralist or structuralist. This lack of clear theoretical foundations is a particular weakness of Mazzucato's argument for the entrepreneurial state as one can raise several questions here. Would a Weberian state (and indeed any other form of state) be able to function as an entrepreneurial state? What are the theoretical presuppositions of such a state given that the Schumpeterian notion of entrepreneurship is strictly focused on individuals and not on political institutions? In her later version of the same argument (published as a book), Mazzucato (2014: 3) explains that the reason why she talks of an 'entrepreneurial state' is that:

> entrepreneurship – what every policy maker today seems to want to encourage – is not (just) about start-ups, venture capital and 'garage thinkers'. It is about the willingness and ability of economic agents to take on risk and real *Knightian* uncertainty: what is genuinely unknown.

However, there are two problems with her explanation. First, Schumpeter would probably reject the idea that entrepreneurship is about taking on risk. In *The Theory of Economic Development* (1983: 137) he argues:

> The entrepreneur is never the risk bearer. . . . The one who gives credit comes to grief if the undertaking fails. For although any property possessed by the entrepreneur may be liable, yet such possession of wealth is not essential, even though advantageous. But even if the entrepreneur finances himself out of former profits, or if he contributes the means of production belonging to his 'static' business, the risk falls on him as capitalist or possessor of goods, not as entrepreneur.

Clearly, if Schumpeter is right in what he argues, then Mazzucato is wrong. That is to say, the state cannot play the role of entrepreneur in Schumpeterian terms but, rather, only finance entrepreneurship through taxation. To put it another way, it is taxpayers who are the risk bearers of innovation. This brings us to the second problem with Mazzucato's argument, which is that the state is not solely an economic agent, it is also a predominantly political one and therefore any state function presupposes political legitimacy. This legitimacy involves a complex process of accepting and justifying the authority of political institutions such as the state to make decisions, including imposing the risk of innovation on taxpayers. The financing of entrepreneurship through taxation, therefore, is not straightforward because it requires political legitimacy and justification, given that there are many other state priorities of redistribution (such as, for example, the financing of health or education through taxation). Mazzucato also seems to confuse the state with government and bureaucracy. For this reason it is difficult for us to tell what kind of political institution she has in mind for the promotion of innovation-led growth.

However, despite these conceptual issues and lack of clear theoretical foundations, Mazzucato's argument is powerful, constituting an implicit political critique of all those who consistently abstract innovation from politics. In a recent review of innovation studies, Steinmueller (2013: 161) admits:

> Our field has an uneasy relationship with public administration as well as politics. No doubt this is partially the consequence of the fact that so many of us are economists, a tribe that paradoxically dominates public administration while at the same time harbouring severe doubts about public purposes.

This admission implies the existence of a problematical epistemology that fails to understand the social and relational nature of radical and/or incremental technological change. Thus, some neo-Schumpeterian economists have difficulty in comprehending innovation in collective and political terms that are guided by bottom-up ethico-political principles of equity, recognition and participation. A decade ago, Edquist (2001) implicitly recognised exactly this problem by accepting that the innovation systems perspective lacked a theory of the state and its role in innovation policy. It might be argued that the reason for this is that neo-Schumpeterian economists adopt a rather positivist approach to technical and technological change. This means that whatever in the innovation process cannot be measured in terms of traditional ST&I indicators, such as R&D expenditure and patents, for example, tends to be dismissed as irrelevant.

Today, however, the innovation process is not only more incremental, involves little or no R&D and often is not patented (Martin, 2013), but it is also more inclusive of developing countries and the poor. The latter engage in public actions and campaigns for producing novel goods and services which meet their basic needs and it is this that we have regarded (Kaplinsky et al., 2009) as 'below the radar innovation' (BRI). BRI challenges the hegemony of established hierarchies in the global innovation processes. It addresses the challenge of meeting the needs of poor consumers through emerging processes of equity, recognition and participation. The impact of ethico-political principles of equity, recognition and participation on BRI can never be measured through the application of positivist methodologies. Such impact is predominately qualitative and long term. As such, it needs to be captured through a set of new indicators able to assess the levels of equity, recognition and participation in relation to new technologies in different sectors.

4.4 Achieving inclusive innovation

Given the role of public action and the importance of politics and the state in the innovation process, achieving inclusivity in the generation and diffusion of new technologies cannot be anything but a political exercise. The question is what kind of politics is in play here. In an earlier work on political theory (Papaioannou, 2014: 117), I broadly defined politics 'as an activity whereby individuals and groups consciously attempt to pursue specific goals such as the preservation or abandonment of social practices and the change or maintenance of social structures and ways of social reproduction'. This broad definition includes government action and formal political systems, but it is not reducible to them. Thus it also includes global public actions and campaigns to change particular social practices of innovation and/or direct them towards justice and wider social transformation.

As they are both local and global social processes, innovation and development drive societies towards (better or worse) conditions of reproduction. It is clear that the inclusivity of these processes depends on whether politics is able not only to assume equity, recognition and participation in social relations of innovation, but also to apply these principles through specific policies, measures and schemes. The problem with mainstream theories of innovation is not only that they ignore the importance of politics in implementing the normative direction of innovation systems, but also that they leave it to the evolutionary process of the free market to decide what this direction should be. Thus, for example, some neo-Schumpeterian economists, such as Metcalfe and Ramlogan (2005), argue for the spontaneous development of knowledge ecologies and innovation ecosystems within the market. Their argument clearly sidelines the importance of politics and the state in the historical emergence of innovation. Instead, it emphasises the problem-solving nature of innovation at a microscale, and the importance of socio-biological evolutionism. Other neo-Schumpeterian thinkers, such as Juma (2016: 28; italics added), insist that:

> Economies are self-organising systems that seek to preserve themselves by precluding transformative ideas. This is necessary to prevent

the system from devolving into chaos. Indeed, Darwinian selection requires that not every mutation be tried. Limiting selection, however, is not always optimal, as favourable mutations will sometimes be overlooked. Technological systems, such as economies and all cultural systems, have built-in stability, but every self-organising system has *mechanisms that can overcome or fool the forces of inertia.*

However, neo-Schumpeterian thinkers in general should be reminded that Schumpeter did not consider the evolutionary process of innovation to be consistently socio-biological. Schumpeter, following Marx, on the one hand argues that capitalism can never be stationary, and on the other insists that economic evolution is not merely a systemic adaptation to changes in external data but rather that it occurs discontinuously and far from smoothly (Schumpeter, 1983). In *The Theory of Economic Development*, Schumpeter (ibid.: 57–58) criticises the continuous enquiry for identifying the 'meaning of history' as metaphysical and argues against conceptions of uniform social development which draw on uncritical analogies with Darwin's theory of evolution. As he says:

> Closely connected with the metaphysical preconception – more precisely with the ideas which grow out of metaphysical roots and become preconceptions if, neglecting unbridgeable gulfs, we make them do the work of empirical science – even if not itself such a metaphysical preconception, is every search for a 'meaning' of history. The same is true of the postulate that a nation, a civilisation, or even the whole of mankind, must show some kind of uniform unilinear development, as even such a matter-of-fact mind as Roscher assumed and as the innumerable philosophers and theorists of history in the long brilliant line from Vico to Lamprecht took and still take for granted. Here, too, belong all kinds of evolutionary thought that centre in Darwin – at least if this means no more than reasoning by analogy – and also the psychological prejudice. . . . But the evolutionary idea is now discredited in our field, especially with historians and ethnologists, for still another reason. To the reproach of unscientific and extra-scientific mysticism that now surrounds the 'evolutionary' ideas, is added that of dilettantism. With all the hasty generalisations in which the word 'evolution plays a part, many of us have lost patience.

Schumpeter's criticism clearly indicates that he is sceptical of the biological tradition as a force of explanation of evolutionary economic phenomena. For him the structure of the problems is not the same in economics and in biology. In *Business Cycles*, Schumpeter (1939: 102) argues that in fact 'evolution is lopsided, discontinuous, disharmonious by nature . . . studded with violent outbursts and catastrophes . . . more like a series of explosions than a gentle, though incessant, transformation'. In this sense, biological metaphors are not applicable and therefore remain irrelevant. What is applicable to understanding economic and technological change is history and institutions. Indeed, as Juma (2016: 27) points out, Schumpeter 'was interested in change over time, which is why he adopted an evolutionary approach that recognised the importance of history'. In doing so, he moved away from (ibid.: 6):

> the classical Darwinian view where innovation arises from mutations whose survival is only guaranteed by the selection environment of the market. This view grants greater agency to the mutant, which in its own right shapes the environment to suit its needs. Technology and institutions are as inseparable as institutions and technology. There is no institution without an element of technology, and the reverse is equally true.

Like Schumpeter, consistent neo-Schumpeterian thinkers such as Freeman (1982, 1987) and Lundvall (1985, 1988) appear to exclude the biological analogy from their evolutionary approach to innovation and technical change. Instead, they deliberately choose a historical method of approach that is designed to illustrate the broad, interactive, relational but also conflictual and discontinuous elements of the system of production, diffusion and use of knowledge and innovation. Geels and Schot (2016) and, before them, Anderson (2009) and Hodgson (1993) accept that the Schumpeterians in the socio-biological tradition of evolution focus narrowly on firms, knowledge, innovation and market selection whereas Freeman keeps 'the broad agenda alive' (Geels & Schot, 2016: 11) and insists on the need to reintegrate economic theory with the other social sciences, including politics, and on the importance of institutional change in innovation. These elements indicate the importance of values, interests and power relations within modern innovation systems. Freeman's and Lundvall's methodological framework is holistic and goes beyond the micro-evolutionary analysis of innovative firm behaviour. According to Freeman and Soete (1997: 17): 'In order to make useful generalisations about R&D in relation to firm behaviour it is essential to place the growth of this phenomenon firmly in a historical context and also in the context of specific industrial sectors'. The macro-evolutionary process of history as such is different from the micro-evolutionary process of biology. While the latter involves the natural selection of genotypic and phenotypic characters taking place behind the backs of social agents, the former involves a continuous conflict of values, material interests and power that takes place in the front of social agents.

The cognitive aspects of agents' decision-making and the dynamic of their systemic interactions have been appreciated by both Freeman and Lundvall in the same way that Schumpeter and Marx appreciated the importance of reason in human action. Indeed, as Hodgson (1993, 2002, 2003) has repeatedly argued, the principal precursors of the socio-biological approach to economics are in fact Thorstein Veblen and Friedrich von Hayek, who applied the Darwinian principles of variation, selection and retention to economic phenomena. Despite evolutionary credentials that are genuine in some broad sense, the same cannot be said for others, including Karl Marx and Joseph Schumpeter. They did not apply the key Darwinian principles to their economics.

Clearly, Hodgson's view of Schumpeter is not shared by economists such as Saviotti and Metcalfe (1991) who discussed the status and prospects of evolutionary theories of economic and technological change, insisting that Schumpeter's approach to innovation contains several elements embedded in modern socio-biological theories of evolution, including in that of Nelson and Winter (1982). The same holds true for a younger generation of evolutionary theorists, such as Geels (2014), who clearly use biological metaphors to explain the domination of certain technologies and innovative designs in the market as well as the domination of cognitive frames or paradigms of analysis. In their view, firms seek to differentiate themselves through product and process innovations which allow them to adapt to economic conditions and be selected within the market in more or less the same way that organisms develop variations in order to adapt to environmental conditions and be naturally selected for survival. According to Saviotti and Metcalfe (1991: 1):

> In biology organisms can reproduce (generally sexually) and pass on their genetic make up to their offspring. The meaning of reproduction is much looser in economics but relates to the maintenance of productive competence over time, and integral to this is the generation and storing of information. Organisations and technologies tend to show some continuity in the course of time, although the pace of change can be much faster and more discontinuous than in biological evolution.

Although discontinuity is clearly recognised by these evolutionary economists as an important element of technological change, their main emphasis remains on the relatively smooth process of the occurrence of the various rule-guided behaviours which become routines within firms. As Nelson and Winter (1982: 97) stress, routines:

> may refer to a repetitive pattern of activity in an entire organisation, to an individual skill, or, as an adjective, to the smooth uneventful effectiveness of such an organisational or individual performance.

More importantly, they claim, routines are analogous to genes. This implies that vital information for organisational survival is stored in routines. Evolution then depends on whether such information enables better adaptation to market conditions and on competitive environments. Dosi (1982, 1988) and other followers of the socio-biological approach to innovation and technical change have built on the notion of 'routines as genes' to introduce the concept of a 'technological paradigm' that, in the words of Dosi and Nelson (1994: 161):

> attempts to capture both the nature of the technological knowledge upon which innovative activities draw and the organisational procedures for the search and exploitation of the innovations.

This concept justifies the modelling of technological change in terms of two determinants: first, that of the 'firms' with the routines which embody the knowledge and information for their survival; second, that of the profitability of a new technology which determines its 'fitness'. Both determinants explain innovation processes at the micro level, failing to account for the complex system of social and political relations at a macro level. The latter has been clearly captured through the notion of innovation systems introduced by more consistent neo-Schumpeterian thinkers such as Freeman and Soete (1997), Lundvall (1992) and Edquist (1997). These thinkers stressed that not only the market mechanism and firms (the micro level) but also the state and politics (the macro level) play key roles in innovation systems. As Freeman and Soete (1997: 14) put it:

> The market mechanism can be a useful technique for allocating resources in certain rather specific circumstances, but it has its limitations, so that the definition and implementation of social priorities for science and technology cannot be left simply to the free play of market forces. . . . The political system is inevitably involved.

As I have stressed elsewhere (Papaioannou et al., 2009), the emphasis from some inconsistent neo-Schumpeterians on socio-biological evolution offers very little towards understanding the specific dynamics of technological innovation. These dynamics are very much political and historical, and they depend on both central and regional government policies. Ignoring not only politics but also history in evolutionary economics, as Perez (2013: 92) stresses, 'is simply unacceptable . . . it would be unthinkable to Freeman but also to Marx and Schumpeter'. Politics reminds us that whether relations of innovation are inclusive or not is a matter of public action and campaigning for equity, recognition and participation. This bottom-up process of politics simply implies various levels of engagement with new and often controversial technologies. As Juma (2016: 292) insists:

> Fundamentally, building local capabilities and fostering public engagement in technology development are critical elements of inclusive innovation. In most cases, opposition to new technology arises from a sense of exclusion. It is about understanding the subtle distinctions between technology as products and technology as platforms for generating new solutions that may not be the priority of the sales departments of foreign firms. It is not a surprise, though, that the absence of inclusive strategies leads to intense debates over questions of justice, equity, corporate control and challenges to intellectual property system.

History teaches us that the process of technical change towards greater inclusion is discontinuous. Since the 1960s and 1970s the world has experienced the Information and Communications Technology (ICT) revolution, the emergence of controversial technologies such as gene editing, artificial intelligence and robotics, increased economic globalisation and the rapid catching up of the developing world. At the same time, whether within advantaged, emerging or developing countries, economic, social and geographical inequalities exist which technological innovation can address provided, that is, its normative direction is politically changed towards greater inclusion.

It is true that, generally speaking, technological innovation has helped the poor to achieve better living standards. But, with new technologies and globalisation disadvantaging many people, the picture is rapidly changing. Thus, as Perez (2013: 94) suggests:

> The idea that there is a technological frontier that is constantly advancing and improving lives may need rethinking if conditions require a reconsideration of what are the most socially relevant directions for innovation.

Such rethinking, however, can only be done in moral and political terms. Overcoming the dogmatic belief in the spontaneous technological advantages of the free market will require first a moral and political critique of the neo-liberal approach to innovation, and then an alternative proposal being put forward for reshaping the economy through public policy. The new thinking already guides public action and campaigning for inclusive innovation. Evolutionary economics and innovation studies need to connect with public actors such as NGOs and social movements. Indeed, as Lundvall (2013) points out, evolutionary economics and innovation studies ought to become more involved in politics and policy in order for them to confront neo-liberal capitalism.

Concluding remarks

Non-ideal principles of equity, recognition and participation in innovation can only be relational and generated through public action and campaigning. Empirical evidence and examples so far indicate that change in structures and policies towards greater inclusion is the result of a social and political struggle. This struggle involves not only civil society organisations, NGOs and social movements but also politics and the state. In the 21st century, more and more of such struggles are seeming to gather momentum, especially in developing countries. As a result, it is not surprising that alternative and more inclusive models of innovations are emerging in the global south (and north). Through grassroots movements and campaigns against unjust innovation, the global south has been successful in managing to offer more inclusive technologies and innovative processes for improving the lives of the poor.

References

Anderson, E. S. (1999) 'What Is the Point of Equality?', *Ethics*, Vol.109, No.2, pp. 287–337.

Anderson, E. S. (2010) *The Imperative of Integration*, Princeton, NJ and Oxford: Princeton University Press.

Anderson, E. S. (2014) 'Reply to Critiques of *The Imperative of Integration*', *Political Studies*, Vol.12, No.3, pp. 345–346.

Block, F. and Keller, M. (2011) *State of Innovation: The US Government's Role in Technology Development*, London: Paradigm Publishers.

Coriat, B. (2015) 'From Exclusive IPR Innovation Regimes to Commons-Based Innovation Regimes: Issues and Perspectives', *Conference Paper*. Available at: www.researchgate.net/publication/283676666 [accessed 26 January 2018].

Dosi, G. (1982) 'Technological Paradigms and Technological Trajectories', *Research Policy*, Vol.11, No.3, pp. 147–162.

Dosi, G. (1988) 'Sources, Procedures and Microeconomic Effects on Innovation', *Journal of Economic Literature*, Vol.26, pp. 126–171.

Dosi, G. and Nelson, R. R. (1994) 'An Introduction to Evolutionary Theories of Economics', *Journal of Evolutionary Economics*, Vol.4, pp. 153–172.

Edquist, C. (1997) *Systems of Innovation: Technologies, Institutions and Organisations*, London: Pinter.

Edquist, C. (2001) 'The Systems of Innovation Approach and Innovation Policy: An Account of the State of the Art', *DRUID Conference Paper*.

Etzkowitz, H. and Leydesdorff, L. (1995) 'The Triple Helix-University-Industry-Government Relations: A Laboratory for Knowledge-Based Economic Development', *EASST Review*, Vol.14, pp. 14–19.

Etzkowitz, H. and Leydesdorff, L. (2000) 'The Dynamics of Innovation: From National Systems and Mode 2 to Triple Helix of University-Industry-Government Relations', *Research Policy*, Vol.29, No.2, pp. 109–123.

Foster, C. and Heeks, R. (2013) 'Conceptualising Inclusive Innovation: Modifying Systems of Innovation Framework to Understand Diffusion of New Technology to Low-Income Consumers', *European Journal of Development Research*, Vol.25, No.3, pp. 333–355.

Freeman, C. (1982) 'Technological Infrastructure and International Competitiveness', draft paper submitted to the OECD ad hoc group on Science, Technology and Competitiveness, August 1982.

Freeman, C. (1987) *Technology Policy and Economic Performance: Lessons from Japan*, London: Pinter.

Freeman, C. and Soete, L. (1997) *The Economics of Industrial Innovation*, London: Pinter.

Geels, F. W. (2014) 'Reconceptualising the Co-Evolution of Firms-in-Industries and Their Environments: Developing an Inter-Disciplinary Triple Embeddedness Framework', *Research Policy*, Vol.43, pp. 261–277.

Geels, F. W. and Schot, J. (2016) 'Towards a New Innovation Theory for Grand Societal Challenges', *Paper for SPRU Anniversary Conference*, 7–9 September 2016, pp. 1–37.

HAI (2012) 'Time for the EU to Lead on Innovation: EU Policy Opportunities in Biomedical Innovation and the Promotion of Public Knowledge Goods', *Policy Paper*. Available at: http://haieurope.org/wp-content/uploads/2012/04/HAI-Europe_TACD-EU-Innovation-Paper.pdf [accessed 26 January 2018].

Hertzberg, B. (2014) 'The Imperative of Integration: Introduction', *Political Studies Review*, Vol.12, No.3, pp. 345–346.

Hodgson, G. M. (1993) *Economics and Evolution: Bringing Life Back into Economics*, Cambridge: Polity Press.

Hodgson, G. M. (2002) 'Darwinism in Economics: From Analogy to Ontology', *Journal of Evolutionary Economics*, Vol.12, pp. 259–281.

Hodgson, G. M. (2003) 'The Mystery of the Routine: The Darwinian Destiny of an Evolutionary Theory of Economic Change', *Revue Économique*, Vol.54, No.2, pp. 355–384.

Juma, C. (2016) *Innovation and Its Enemies: Why People Resist New Technologies*, Oxford: Oxford University Press.

Kaplinsky, R., Chataway, J., Clark, N., Hanlin, R., Kale, D., Muraguri, L., Papaioannou, T., Robbins, P. and Wamae, W. (2009) 'Below the Radar: What Does Innovation in Emerging Economies Have to Offer Other Low-Income Economies?', *International Journal of Technology Management & Sustainable Development*, Vol.8, No.3, pp. 177–197.

KEI (2009) 'Comments of Knowledge Ecology International (KEI) to the WHO Public Hearing for Proposals for New and Innovative Sources of Funding to Stimulate R&D'. Available at: www.who.int/phi/KEI.pdf [accessed 26 January 2018].

Lundvall, B.-A. (1985) *Product Innovation and User-Producer Interaction*, Aalborg: Aalborg University Press.

Lundvall, B.-A. (1988) 'Innovation as an Interactive Process: From User-Producer Interaction to the National System of Innovation', in G. Dosi (ed.), *Technical Change and Economic Theory*, London and New York: Pinter.

Lundvall, B.-A. (ed.) (1992) *National Systems of Innovation: Towards a Theory of Innovation and Interactive Learning*, London: Pinter

Lundvall, B.-A. (2013) 'Innovation Studies: A Personal Interpretation of the State of the Art', in J. Fagerberg, B. R. Martin and E. S. Andersen (eds.), *Innovation Studies: Evolution and Future Challenges*, Oxford: Oxford University Press.

Martin, B. R. (2013) 'Innovation Studies: An Emerging Agenda', in J. Fagerberg, B. R. Martin and E. S. Andersen (eds.), *Innovation Studies: Evolution and Future Challenges*, Oxford: Oxford University Press.

Mazzucato, M. (2011) *The Entrepreneurial State*, London: DEMOS.

Mazzucato, M. (2014) *The Entrepreneurial State: Debunking Public vs. Private Sector Myths*, London: Anthem Press.

Metcalfe S, and Ramlogan R, 2005 "Innovation Systems and the Competitive Process in Developing Countries", Paper Prepared for *Regulation, Competition and Income Distribution: Latin American Experiences*, a Joint Conference Organised and Sponsored by the University of Illinois (University of Manchester and University of Sao Paulo, Paraty, Brazil).

MSF (2011) *Medical Innovations in Humanitarian Situations: The Work of Médecins Sans Frontières*. Available at: www.msf.org.au/fileadmin/specialfeatures/medical_innovations/medinnovbk.pdf [accessed 26 January 2018].

Nelson, R. R. and Winter, S. G. (1982) *An Evolutionary Theory of Economic Change*, Cambridge, MA: Harvard University Press.

Papaioannou, T. (2014) 'How Inclusive Can Innovation for Development Be in the 21st Century?', *Journal of Innovation and Development*, Special Issue: New Models of Inclusive Innovation for Development, Vol.4, No.2, pp. 187–202.

Papaioannou, T., Wield, D. and Chataway, J. (2009) 'Knowledge Ecologies and Ecosystems? An Empirically Grounded Reflection on Recent Developments in Innovation Systems Theory', *Environment and Planning C: Government and Policy*, Vol.27, No.2, pp. 319–339.

Perez, C. (2013) 'Innovation Systems and Policy for Development in a Changing World', in J. Fagerberg, B. R. Martin and E. S. Andersen (eds.), *Innovation Studies: Evolution and Future Challenges*, Oxford: Oxford University Press.

Piketty, T. (2014) *Capital in the Twenty-First Century*, Harvard: Belknap Press.

Rawls, J. (1972) *A Theory of Justice*, Oxford: Oxford University Press.

Saviotti, P. P. and Metcalfe, J. S. (eds.) (1991) *Evolutionary Theories of Economic and Technological Change*, Chur, Reading, Paris, Philadelphia, Tokyo and Melbourne: Harwood Academic Publishers.

Schumpeter, J. A. (1939) *Business Cycles: A Theoretical, Historical and Statistical Analysis of the Capitalist Process*, New York: McGraw-Hill.

Schumpeter, J. A. (1983) *The Theory of Economic Development*, New Brunswick and London: Transaction Publishers.

Smith, A., Fressoli, M., Abrol, D., Arond, E. and Ely, A. (2017) *Grassroots Innovation Movements*, London and New York: Routledge.

Smith, A. and Stirling, A. (2018) 'Innovation, Sustainability and Democracy: An Analysis of Grassroots Contributions', *Journal of Self-Governance and Management Economics*, Vol.6, No.1, pp. 64–97.

Smith, A., Voß, J.-P. and Grin, J. (2010) 'Innovation Studies and Sustainability Transitions: The Allure of the Multi-Level Perspective and Its Challenges', *Research Policy*, Vol.39, pp. 435–448.

Steinmueller, W. E. (2013) 'Innovation Studies at Maturity', in J. Fagerberg, B. R. Martin and E. S. Andersen (eds.), *Innovation Studies: Evolution and Future Challenges*, Oxford: Oxford University Press.

Thomas, H., Fressoli, M. and Becerra, L. (2012) 'Science and Technology Policy and Social Ex/Inclusion: Analysing Opportunities and Constraints in Brazil and Argentina', *Science and Public Policy*, Vol.39, pp. 579–591.

Timmermann, Cristian (2013), *Life Sciences, Intellectual Property Regimes and Global Justice*. PhD thesis, Wageningen University. Available at: http://edepot.wur.nl/276714 [accessed 25 April 2018]

Wolff, J. (2012) *The Human Right to Health*, New York and London: W. W. Norton & Company.

Young, I. M. (1990) *Justice and the Politics of Difference*, Princeton, NJ: Princeton University Press.

Young, I. M. (2001) 'Activist Challenges to Deliberative Democracy', *Political Theory*, Vol.29, pp. 670–690.

Young, I. M. (2011) *Responsibility for Justice*, Oxford and New York: Oxford University Press.

Ypi, L. (2012) *Global Justice and Avant-Garde Political Agency*, Oxford: Oxford University Press.

5 Evaluating inclusive innovation in terms of non-ideal principles

Throughout this book I have argued that achieving inclusive innovation is predominantly a political process that follows principles of equity, recognition and participation generated from the bottom up. These principles ought to guide not only access to innovative goods and services in health, food, energy, housing and transport, for example, but also their social production by means of both capital and labour. The question that next arises is whether we can effectively assess inclusive innovation in terms of social relations of equity, recognition and participation. What would a non-ideal framework of inclusive innovation look like? How should processes, outcomes and impacts of innovation be evaluated? Is there any possibility of establishing equitable and participatory innovation systems? What does it mean, after all, to meet the demands of justice in innovation? The following sections can only briefly touch upon these questions by outlining an evaluative approach to inclusive innovation. Full exploration would require an entire book on the topic. The argument I shall put forward here is that existing methodologies and methods of evaluation such as innovation benchmarking can be updated and/or adapted in such a way that they are able to measure inclusiveness in the innovation process. However, this adaptation should take place with the involvement of all stakeholders, including innovators, regulators and communities that were previously excluded. If the broad idea of inclusive innovation is that no one ought to be left behind, then new indicators ought to be democratically agreed by all agents of social change.

5.1 A non-ideal framework of inclusive innovation

The assumption that there is a trickle-down effect from high innovation performance and economic growth to social inclusion has proven illusory. As Alzugaray et al. (2012: 117) point out:

> even the blending of improved economic conditions and focused social policies have left important parts of the population in many countries

without access to dignified life conditions. . . . Equally illusory is the hypothesis that with greater scientific and technological achievements, we will be capable of solving the social exclusion problems that our societies face.

The reason for this is that inclusion cannot be achieved unless the social relations of innovative production are recognised, democratised and equalised. But what does this mean in practice? Production as such delivers technical solutions to problems within sectors including health, food and transport. These solutions can reach people and satisfy equally their basic needs as long as people are recognised not only as consumers but also as users who can be involved equally and participate democratically in the innovation production process itself, promoting the agency of the excluded. Such participation implies an absence of hierarchies and oppressions in the relations of knowledge generation and utilisation for the meeting of basic needs. It also implies an absence of unequal structures such as IPRs and the development of better institutional frameworks of interaction and knowledge sharing.

Because innovation is predominately a social process, it needs to be evaluated as such. Evaluation is a social construction but one that is crucial for policymakers, investors and analysts who want to move from a normative theory to action, based on evidence about what really works in the area of inclusive innovation. However, traditional evaluative frameworks remain linear; they mainly use R&D expenditure and investment as input indicators and patents and publications data as output indicators of knowledge and innovation generation. These traditional indicators are provided by manuals such as the commonly known OECD, Frascati and Patent Manuals (Papaioannou, 2003), which focus on innovation for economic growth. Along with innovation surveys, mainly based on the Oslo Manual (OECD, 1997), they measure top-down innovation activities in a hierarchical way, thus failing to grasp the degrees of inclusivity and interactivity of emerging innovation systems, especially in developing countries. In a number of cases, traditional indicators of innovation even become policy targets. In so doing, they open the door to manipulation and cease to provide relevant information content.

The continuing application of traditional indicators in evaluating the innovation performance of developing (and developed) countries has meant that transformative non-hierarchical models of low- and high-tech innovation based on indigenous knowledge and bottom-up principles of equity, participation and recognition have been completely overlooked. In countries such as Brazil, Cuba, Uruguay and also in South Africa, China and India, grassroots and/or frugal innovations involve the private sector and NGOs and local communities in innovative production that succeeds in meeting basic needs in a socially just way. For example, Jayaashree Industries, a company which produces sanitary napkin machines in India, sells its products to self-help groups around the country to meet the needs of poor women in rural areas at a low cost, while mobile health and education Apps in Kenya and South Africa such as ChildCount+ and Project Masiluleke improve the lives of thousands of patients in these countries. Further examples are offered by M-Pess and micro-saving and micro-credit innovations in African countries and India which enable poor people to meet their basic financial needs, as well as Terrasys Energy in Indonesia, which, through hydroelectricity production techniques, distributes electricity in remote areas (OECD, 2015).

Although such innovations transform people's lives, they are treated by mainstream innovation studies as marginal simply because they cannot be measured by existing frameworks of evaluation. These frameworks are predominantly quantitative, claiming both universality and objectivity, and their claims are based on an epistemological illusion of value-neutrality that abstracts innovation from particular social contexts and development processes. Some (rather inconsistent) neo-Schumpeterian thinkers promote value-neutrality and universality throughout their writings, essentially defending scientism in innovation and development studies. In their view, innovation can be positioned as if it were a value-neutral process of supply and demand, taking place in a free market and having nothing to do with politics and the political state and government. Following their thinking, innovation can be modelled in terms of two determinants: first, the 'firms' with their routines which embody the knowledge and information necessary for their survival; second, the profitability of a new technology that determines its 'fitness'. Both determinants explain innovation processes at a micro level, failing to account for the complex and contradictory system of social and political relations at the macro level. The framework is thus based on mechanisms of co-ordination, adaptation and selection, as if the market were a socio-biological organism rather than a historically developed institution founded upon a political state that protects exploitative relations of individual property rights and guarantees capitalist forms of economic exchange based on supply and demand. However, as Commons (1924) and later Penrose (1952) have pointed out, institutional evolution involves 'artificial' selection. Their argument implies that human (both individual and collective) action is guided not only by economic values and material interests but also by moral and political values. There is no such thing as pure calculative behaviour, despite its having been mistakenly privileged by neoclassical economic theory as *Homo Economicus* (Tsakalotos, 2005). Economic values and material interests require justifications through normative debates. As Tsakalotos (ibid.: 896) points out: 'Norms and values do not just help us to achieve better goals which are already adhered to, they also determine the kind of people we are or want to become'.

Alternative evaluative frameworks based on the normative principles of equity, participation and recognition are predominantly qualitative, focusing on local social relations of innovation. Within such frameworks, assessments of innovation products and services in terms of their fitness to increase inclusion can move beyond input and output indicators and towards the normative demands of justice. These are, in essence, demands of inclusivity of people's needs in the very social relations of innovation. The informational basis for assessments of inclusive innovation can mainly be founded upon people's feedback on the processes, outcomes and impacts of innovation in informal settings (Cozzens & Sutz, 2014). For example, equitable innovation processes can be indicated by equal knowledge sharing and the absence of oppressive relations and/or hierarchies in the value chains of new technologies, whether these be in health, food, energy, housing or transport; measures of affordable access to quality, sustainable goods and services can be used to provide a holistic view of equitable innovation; and democratic participation can be indicated by public engagement in specific processes of innovation and inclusion of the poor in value chains, making sure that the outcomes of these processes are socially desirable and risks are minimised. Additional measures may include types of public engagement and the freedom to co-produce inclusive innovations. Recognition can be indicated by innovative products and processes which satisfy the basic needs of previously excluded and/or misrecognised social groups. For these groups recognition is presupposed of any inclusion in innovation. This is, for example, the reason why: 'The HBN deliberately chose the idea of individual grassroots innovators as knowledge-rich, economically poor individuals who were deprived of recognition, respect and reward' (Smith et al., 2017: 151).

Until now, given the dominance of traditional indicators for measuring innovation, public policy has been formulated on the basis of incorrect scientific evidence. In the process it has reproduced existing top-down structures of innovation which fail to meet the needs of either the poor or marginalised people. Existing innovation systems lack the analytical tools and methods to evaluate their inclusive (or exclusive) processes, outputs and impacts. There is therefore an urgent need for a shift towards more normative judgements that are informed by evidence from non-ideal innovation contexts. This is not to say that the collection of statistics is no longer relevant. On the contrary, both national and regional statistics can give very relevant data, provided we ask questions that go beyond R&D and patents. Indeed, traditional indicators and measures of innovation have been extensively criticised for their narrow focus on input and output because, as such, they are unable to capture processes and outcomes of inclusive innovation.

The current production paradigm requires reassessment and new indicators should be introduced that are able to measure progress with the ultimate objective of greater inclusive innovation. As Cassiolato and Soares (2015: 22) argue:

> Successful cases involve people as protagonists in user innovation, drawing in their experience and knowledge to design solutions according to their needs. For example, [in agriculture] participation by poor people has proven critical for diffusing soil conservation techniques, capturing rain water in semi-arid areas, and using ICTs in basic education.

In health, the realisation that inequality and poverty are sources of illnesses has led to the social development of innovative pharmaceutical products and medical devices which treat diseases neglected by the mainstream R&D establishment (Sutz, 2015).

One successful example of this is that of the Cuban vaccine against the Hib (Haemophilus influenzae type b) bacteria. Hib is responsible for 386,000 deaths every year, almost all of which are children under 5 years old. According to Astronomo and Burton (2010: 316):

> In 1989, a team from Cuba embarked on a project to produce a new, more economical conjugate anti-Hib vaccine from a fully synthetic capsular polysaccharide antigen. In collaboration with a Canadian chemist they spent 2 years developing a streamlined synthetic scheme that is amenable to large scale production. . . . The antigen was first conjugated to human serum albumin (HSA) for antigenic evaluation and then to tetanus toxoid (TT) for immunogenicity studies in animals and finally clinical studies in adults, children and infants. Fourteen years and seventeen clinical trials later, the result is a 99.7% success rate in children.

The Cuban vaccine against Hib is clearly a scarcity-induced innovation (Srinivas & Sutz, 2008) that increases health inclusion and promotes social justice.

Another example is that of the blue light lamp used in Uruguay for the phototherapy of newborn children with strong jaundice (Sutz, 2015). Although different types of blue light lamps are already available in the market (such as halogen bulbs, which can tend to burn out quite frequently, and light-emitting diode – LED – lamps, which offer low intensity), none of the existing models are practical and/or affordable in a developmental context (Alzugaray et al., 2012). The solution was provided by an Uruguayan physicist who used (Sutz, 2015: 100):

> ten times less LEDs by including an optical device that multiplies the light intensity of an array of LEDs. The relation of this issue to social inclusion derives from the fact that premature babies are more prone to have this disease; the proportion of premature babies is notoriously higher among those whose mothers are poor, and particularly poor teenage girls. Those mothers gave birth in public hospitals; for these hospitals having access to a blue light lamp of good performance is key to treating premature babies with severe jaundice; before this solution was found, lamp scarcity was a real problem.

Sutz classifies both examples as frugal innovations which, by responding to scarce resources, address problems of inclusion. But, in fact, what these inclusive innovations have in common is that they cannot be evaluated in terms of traditional indicators such as R&D and patents. Thus, as Sutz (ibid.) correctly stresses:

> They are rather invisible, given that the type of innovation scrutiny we usually perform does not recognise them; they mainly consist of surveys, even if service innovation surveys have begun to spread out. But they are rather invisible for other reasons too; mainly because the innovators themselves do not recognise their activity to innovate.

To illustrate the problem of the invisibility of inclusive innovations, Sutz provides us with the example of clinicians at the University Hospital in Uruguay. According to her (ibid.: 101), when they:

> were asked about innovations in their practices . . . their answers indicated that there were eventually few. But when going from one specialty to another, talking in more detail with clinicians, home-made solutions to the problems they were facing often appeared, including physical devices they have invented, fabricated and introduced their practice.

This problem of the invisibility of inclusive innovations is crucial from a policy perspective. In order for policy to promote inclusive innovation, there is need for evidence that simply cannot be provided through the existing evaluative frameworks. What is required is that equity, participation and recognition be used as an alternative framework for evaluating the processes and outcomes of inclusive innovation. Only this new framework will be able to raise awareness among policymakers and practitioners of the importance of inclusive innovative solutions to pressing technological problems.

5.2 Evaluating processes, outcomes and impacts of inclusive innovation

To argue that a process and/or an outcome and/or an impact of innovation is inclusive presupposes a much more detailed set of indicators and measures. What is it exactly that indicates that equity, participation and recognition have been achieved in relations of the innovative production of new goods and services? Where does an acceptable threshold for equal allocation of resources, opportunities and/or capabilities, and democratic participation and recognition lie? A non-ideal theory of inclusive innovation should necessarily lead to a non-ideal evaluative framework of inclusive innovation. This means that existing indicators and measures should be updated from the bottom up through discussion and critical appraisal by all the different stakeholders, including public actors, campaigners and the users and producers of inclusive innovation. Such a framework might, in turn, facilitate the development of a new set of bottom-up policies that are able to promote and support inclusive innovation. However, so far very few researchers have made the effort to outline a non-ideal evaluative framework of inclusive innovation. Among those that have, Heeks et al. (2013) recognise the multi-dimensional character of inclusiveness and provide a 'ladder of inclusive innovation' with six levels, each of which represents an increase in inclusive innovation. The six levels are:

- Level 1: **Intention** of addressing the needs of the excluded group;
- Level 2: **Consumption** of innovation by the excluded group;
- Level 3: **Positive impact** of innovation on the livelihoods of the excluded group;
- Level 4: **Process** of innovation that involves the excluded group;
- Level 5: **Structure** of innovation that needs to be inclusive; and
- Level 6: **Post-structure** of innovation that is inclusive if it is created within an inclusive frame of knowledge.

This ladder of inclusive innovation could lead to different indicators of intention, consumption, impact, process, structure and post-structure of inclusiveness. However, the purpose of Heeks et al. (ibid.) at the time of their publishing it in 2013 was conceptual clarification rather than measurement. It was a further two years before Foster and Heeks seem to have proposed five indicators that were able to capture the main causes of inclusive innovation failure and thereby justify policy intervention. These were: 1) *formal innovations focus insufficiently on the poor*; 2) *informal actors are delinked from innovation systems*; 3) *those serving peripheral markets have weak adaptive capacity*; 4) *low-income users lack capability to use innovations effectively*; 5) *underlining policies and context are weak or absent* (Foster & Heeks, 2015: 4; italics added).

Foster and Heeks, however, do not deduce their evaluative outline from a comprehensive theory of inclusive innovation founded upon the relational notions of equity, participation and recognition. In this sense, they are unable to justify their indicators on the grounds of non-ideal principles of justice. While the empirical foundation of their outline is sound, it fails to oblige public policy to achieve objectives such as the reorientation of innovation systems towards the poor, reduction of structural barriers to inclusive innovation, effective use of innovations among low-income groups and improvement of the absorptive capacity of low-income groups (ibid.). Nevertheless, Foster and Heeks are able to suggest specific policy instruments for each of these objectives and refer readers to their previous work to find benchmarks for inclusive innovation (Heeks et al., 2013). The policy instruments they put forward target three aspects of inclusive innovation (ibid.: 21–22):

> readiness (that is the foundations and precursors that input to innovation process); innovation (the process of innovation itself); and impact of inclusive innovation. Measuring the process of inclusive innovation will be very challenging and likely labour intensive, involving regular on-the-ground surveys. The same could be true of impact measurement.

Indeed, especially when it comes to impact measurement, the challenges involve the epistemological and methodological processes of analysing and monitoring the intended and unintended consequences of inclusive innovation. In addition, collecting robust data for impact indicators can prove difficult because it involves obtaining qualitative feedback from a representative sample of low-income populations within a particular period of historical time.

In a recent paper, van der Merwe and Grobbelaar (2016) recognise the difficulties with measuring the impact of innovation on excluded groups as well as the lack of empirically validated indicators and performance measures for inclusive innovation systems. In response to this they suggest impact research could use conventional economic indicators to assess the impact on livelihoods. In addition, they seek to develop a more comprehensive analytical framework than that of Heeks et al. (2013) to measure inclusive innovation systems. Van der Merwe's and Grobbelaar's framework involves five steps. The first is definition of the innovation system focus, which should be clear in terms of analysis and focus of inclusion. Also systemic boundaries are important to consider whether the measurement is around a particular product, service, industry, sector or region. The second step is a structural approach that includes two sub-steps: identification of the structural components of inclusive innovation systems and a functional approach. Within these sub-steps, actors, interactions, knowledge, innovation institutions and infrastructure are measured by several indicators including 'marginalised actors' involvement', 'informal relations' and 'local knowledge'. The third step concerns a system failure approach and inducement and blocking mechanisms. Identifying insufficiencies in the functioning of the innovation system that lead to exclusivity and marginalisation is crucial to evaluation. Also, identifying the obstacles caused by the innovation system functions can impact positively on improving inclusivity. Innovation systems include functions such as the entrepreneurial, knowledge generation and dissemination. Problems including, for example, inadequate interaction, knowledge and learning can reduce inclusiveness. Van der Merwe and Grobbelaar (ibid.) develop sets of indicators for all the identified functions of innovation systems. Step four, meanwhile, concerns assessing the functionality of the inclusive innovation system and adjusting a phase of development to incorporate the 'inclusive innovation ladder' of Heeks et al. (2013). Finally, step five concerns policies for inclusive innovation. Greater inclusion requires policies which are able to move beyond traditional innovation systems. These can be both vertical and horizontal innovation policies. According to van der Merwe and Grobbelaar (2016: 354), inclusive innovation:

> fosters a need to consider the whole lifecycle of invention, innovation, diffusion and how actors in the system learn when establishing policies. For each policy the major challenges are to measure (i.e. objectives) how it is implemented (i.e. instruments) and towards which actors it is targeted (i.e. institutions). Policies are oriented towards several objectives, instruments and/or institutions. For objectives and policy goals a clear set of instruments and institutions should be available to achieve the objectives through implementation of policies.

Apart from the difficulties of collecting robust data for measurement, one should also consider whether key principles of inclusive innovation benchmarking (Papaioannou et al., 2006) can be adopted and applied in van der Merwe's and Grobbelaar's analytical framework given their lack of a comprehensive theory of inclusive innovation. Take, for example, the principle of focus that these authors also endorse. According to Papaioan-nou et al. (ibid.: 93), 'Benchmarking requires a clear focus – the tighter the definition of the core process being studied, the more valuable and focused the learning opportunities'. In van der Merwe's and Grobbelaar's frame-work, however, it is unclear whether the focus is on inclusive innovation as a bottom-up participatory process for addressing equally the basic needs of groups recognised for their exclusion, or whether it is on inclusive innova-tion as a top-down mechanism for reducing social exclusion and increasing the positive impact on the livelihoods of excluded groups. Clarifying this (and further points) is crucial if a plausible evaluative framework that can compete with traditional manuals and succeed in influencing policy and practice is to be developed.

5.3 Equitable and participatory innovation systems

As I have already implied, evaluating inclusive innovation presupposes tak-ing on board the principles and steps of existing methodologies and meth-ods of evaluation. Indeed, innovation benchmarking is one such step that can be updated and modified for the purpose of serving as a tool for evalu-ation. Benchmarking indicates a structured comparison between innova-tion processes that, by offering a starting point from which to gauge higher standards of inclusiveness and/or cases of inclusive innovation, can enable learning concerning how best to close the gap (Papaioannou et al., 2006). Indeed as Auluck (2002: 111) has pointed out, 'Benchmarking is a continu-ous process of identifying, understanding and adapting practice and pro-cesses that will lead to better performance'. Better performance in terms of inclusive innovation implies identifying, understanding, and adapting practices and processes of equity, recognition and participation. In turn, this can facilitate learning about how performance differences come about in different contexts, including that of developing countries.

Focusing on questions of 'how' and 'what' enables useful imitation and configuration of inclusive innovation structures, methods and procedures, and can help to promote better policies for inclusive innovation. Inclusive innovation benchmarking can be both a performance- and a process-based exercise. In addition, it can follow a number of key principles: *focus* (clear focus on the core process of inclusive innovation); *differentiation* (clear dis-tinction between the dimensions of the performance and practice of inclusive-ness); *measurement* (objective measures of inclusive innovation systems); *learning* (critical discussion of results); *comparability* (ensuring that the gaps between the innovation processes studied are not too large); *integration* (evaluation should be incorporated into a more integrated framework of jus-tice); and *applicability* (inclusive innovation benchmarking can be applied both across sectors and internationally) (Papaioannou et al., 2006).

Given these methodological principles, any exercise to evaluate innovation processes in terms of equity, recognition and participation should be concerned with input/output/impact. This is to suggest that an innovation can be considered to be inclusive if inputs (such as knowledge and resources), outputs (such as novel goods and services), and impacts (such as increase of human capabilities and improvement of livelihoods) are equally shared and involve the democratic participation of people who are recognised for rights to satisfy their basic needs. Once such conditions are in place then there is good evidence to indicate that the social relations in the specific innovation process concerned are those of equality rather than those of domination and/or oppression.

At this point it might be stressed that equitable and participatory innovation systems tend always to be inclusive. This means that their normative direction is always towards making poor people better off in a socially just way. In order to do this, they promote bottom-up frugal and/or grassroots innovations and facilitate effective use of innovative goods and services among the poor. In addition to this, as Foster and Heeks (2015) correctly point out, inclusive innovation systems allow for the removal of economic, social, political or spatial barriers that might prevent or limit the potential for inclusive innovations, actors and learning. But, as I have repeatedly emphasised in this book, innovation systems are not abstract formations; rather they are embedded in wider social and political contexts. As a result, moral and political norms influence the extent to which they can be inclusive.

The bottom-up principles of equity, participation and recognition which have been morally and politically defended in this book are predominantly redistributive. From this it follows that equitable and participatory innovation systems are redistributive of resources, welfare and/or capabilities. For example, given that inclusive innovation systems such as grassroots and frugal innovations invariably require additional financial and organisational support for their commercialisation (especially in the case of medical devices and medicines), as well as support for their documentation, standardisation and scaling up, for the sake of inclusion equitable and participatory innovation systems ought to address these requirements. In this way, no one should be left worse off in terms of meeting his or her basic needs through a new good or service.

5.4 Meeting the demands of justice

Justice does not only pay in one 'currency'. The reason being that justice is a multi-dimensional concept. Thus, for example, it demands that rights, opportunities, resources and capabilities are distributed according to bottom-up principles of equity, participation and recognition to ensure that social relations are just. I have argued that in order to meet the demands of justice, the input, output and impact of innovation ought to be inclusive of people and places, satisfying basic human needs. This implies that the normative direction of both existing and emerging innovation systems ought to be moving towards the equalising of social relations in knowledge production and eliminating an innovation-led poverty and inequality that is unjust and arbitrary. The achievement of such fundamental systemic change is in the interests of social, economic and environmental sustainability, as Schot and Steinmueller (2016) point out. However, it cannot come about through transformative innovation policies (ibid.) alone, but public actions and campaigns for transformative change will also be necessary.

As I have repeatedly stressed throughout this book, poverty and inequality are not only morally and politically disturbing, they also pose a fundamental challenge to sustainable growth and prosperity in the 21st century. Clearly, top-down technological innovation has been a major contributing factor to the growing divide between rich and poor (Chataway et al., 2014). Evidence suggests that the framing of science and technology in market terms that are abstracted from moral and political principles has been a serious barrier to its usefulness in eliminating innovation-led poverty and inequality, especially in developing countries. Currently, there is a gulf between innovation and justice. Innovation is largely conducted in a separate sphere from moral and political efforts aimed at tackling major injustices and developmental challenges in areas such as health, agriculture and energy. As a result, it therefore misses its objectives, excludes the poorer segments of the population, and fails to address inequality and the potential for long-term socio-economic development (Arocena & Sutz, 2000; Papaioannou, 2014; Cozzens & Kaplinsky, 2009). The creation of new products and processes which meet the demands of justice (and thereby foster inclusion in production and consumption as well as long-term social and economic benefits), not only presupposes that society's institutions work together to produce just outcomes (Barry, 2005) but, more importantly, that civil society organisations and social movements engage in public action and campaigns for inclusive innovation. The latter approach challenges the liberal presumption that all citizens are equal before the law and, as such, possess equal rights to have their needs recognised and to participate in the satisfaction of these needs. Instead, inclusive innovation places greater emphasis on the equal opportunities or capabilities of people to exercise these rights. In this sense, it is a bottom-up process that aims not only at technical and technological change, but also at radical social and political change that leads towards a fairer society. However, despite what Schot and Steinmueller (2016) seem to suggest, this process does not need to be entirely experimental. As we know already which innovation pathways are not fit for purpose in meeting the demands of social justice, efforts can be shifted to those emerging inclusive innovation pathways which do promote equity, participation and recognition.

Concluding remarks

Evaluating inclusive innovation in terms of non-ideal principles of equity, recognition and participation presupposes a clear framework of alternative indicators. Measurements should focus on whether the processes/outcome/impact of innovation satisfy these principles and also identify the gaps that need to be closed through policy and practice. To achieve this a methodology of inclusive innovation benchmarking should be adopted. Inclusive innovation systems can only ever be those which are equitable, participatory and in which the rights of all stakeholders are recognised and respected. Justice is a multi-currency and relational process that should leave no one worse off in terms of meeting his or her needs.

References

Alzugaray, S., Mederos, L. and Sutz, J. (2012) 'Building Bridges: Social Inclusion Problems as Research and Innovation', *Review of Policy Research*, Vol.29, No.6, pp. 776–796.

Arocena, R. and Sutz, J. (2000) 'Looking at National Systems of Innovation from the South', *Industry and Innovation*, Vol.7, No.1, pp. 55–75.

Astronomo, R. and Burton, D. (2010) 'Carbohydrate Vaccines: Developing Sweet Solutions to Sticky Situations?', *Nature Reviews*, Vol.9, No.4, April, pp. 308–324.

Auluck, R. (2002) 'Benchmarking: A Tool for Facilitating Organisational Learning', *Public Administration and Development*, Vol.22, No.2, pp. 109–122.

Barry, B. (2005) *Why Social Justice Matters*, Cambridge: Polity Press.

Cassiolato, J. E. and Soares, M. C. (eds.) (2015) *Health Innovation Systems, Equity and Development*, Rio de Janeiro: E-papers Serviços Editoriais.

Chataway, J., Hanlin, R. and Kaplinsky, R. (2014) 'Inclusive Innovation: An Architecture for Policy Development', *Innovation and Development*, Vol.4, No.1, pp. 33–54.

Commons, J. R. (1924) *Legal Foundations of Capitalism*, New York: Macmillan.

Cozzens, S. E. and Kaplinsky, R. (2009) 'Innovation, Poverty and Inequality: Cause, Coincidence or Co-Evolution?', in B.-A. Lundvall, K. J. Joseph, C. Chaminade and J. Vang (eds.), *Handbook of Innovation Systems and Developing Countries: Building Domestic Capabilities in a Global Setting*, Cheltenham and Northampton: Edward Elgar.

Cozzens, S. E. and Sutz, J. (2014) 'Innovation in Informal Settings', *Innovation and Development*, Vol.4, No.1, pp. 5–31.

Foster, C. and Heeks, R. (2015) 'Policies to Support Inclusive Innovation', *Development Informatics Working Paper Series No.61*. Available at: http://hummedia.manchester.ac.uk/institutes/gdi/publications/workingpapers/di/di_wp61.pdf [accessed 26 January 2018].

Heeks, R., Amalia, M., Kintu, R. and Shah, N. (2013) 'Inclusive Innovation: Definition, Conceptualisation and Future Research Priorities', *Development Informatics Working Paper Series No.53*. Available at: http://themimu.info/sites/themimu.info/files/documents/Ref_Doc_Definition_Conceptualisation_Future_Research_Priorities_2013.pdf [accessed 26 January 2018].

OECD (1997) *Oslo Manual: Proposed Guidelines for Collecting and Interpreting Technological Innovation Data*, Paris: OECD and Development Statistical Office of the European Communities.

OECD (2015) *Innovation Policies for Inclusive Development: Scaling up Inclusive Innovations*. Available at: www.oecd.org/innovation/inno/scaling-up-inclusive-innovations.pdf [accessed 26 January 2018].

Papaioannou, T. (2003) 'Benchmarking Centres of Excellence and the OECD Manuals of Science and Technology Measurement', in B. Borsi, G. Papanek and T. Papaioannou (eds.), *Towards the Practice of Benchmarking RTD Organisations in the Accession States*, Budapest: Budapest University Press.

Papaioannou, T. (2014) 'How Inclusive Can Innovation for Development Be in the 21st Century?', *Journal of Innovation and Development*, Special Issue: New Models of Inclusive Innovation for Development, Vol.4, No.2, pp. 187–202.

Papaioannou, T., Rush, H. and Bessant, J. (2006) 'Benchmarking as a Policy-Making Tool: From the Private Sector to the Public Sector', *Science and Public Policy*, Vol.33, No.2, pp. 91–102.

Penrose, E. T. (1952) 'Biological Analogies in the Theory of the Firm', *American Economic Review*, Vol.42, No.4, pp. 804–819.

Schot, J. and Steinmueller, W. E. (2016) 'Framing Innovation Policy for Transformative Change: Innovation Policy 3.0', *Science Policy Research Unit (SPRU)*, University of Sussex. Available at: www.johanschot.com/wordpress/wp-content/uploads/2016/09/Framing-Innovation-Policy-for-Transformative-Change-Innovation-Policy-3.0-2016.pdf [accessed 26 January 2018].

Smith, A., Fressoli, M., Abrol, D., Arond, E. and Ely, A. (2017) *Grassroots Innovation Movements*, London and New York: Routledge.

Srinivas, S. and Sutz, J. (2008) 'Developing Countries and Innovation: Searching for a New Analytical Approach', *Technology and Society*, Vol.30, No.2, pp. 129–140.

Sutz, J. (2015) 'Is There a Role for Innovation in Health Equity?', in J. E. Cassiolato and M. C. Soares (eds.), *Health Innovation Systems, Equity and Development*, Rio de Janeiro: E-papers Serviços Editoriais.

Tsakalotos, E. (2005) 'Homo Economicus and the Reconstruction of Political Economy: Six Theses on the Role of Value in Economics', *Cambridge Journal of Economics*, Vol.29, No.6, pp. 893–908.

van der Merwe, E. and Grobelaar, S. S. (2016) 'Evaluating Inclusive Innovation Performance: The Case of the e-Health System of the Western Cape Region, South Africa', *Proceedings of PICMET '16: Technology Management for Social Innovation*. Available at: www.picmet.org/db/member/proceedings/2016/data/polopoly_fs/1.3251671.1472158169!/fileserver/file/680899/filename/16R0435.pdf [accessed 26 January 2018].

Conclusion

This small book has emphasised the need for a theory of justice in innovation. Furthermore, it has attempted to outline such a theory in political terms, in particular by defending the non-ideal principles of equity, recognition and participation as bottom-up principles that are generated through public action and campaigning for justice in innovation. Its main argument has been that these principles can guide the direction of contemporary innovation systems towards equalising social relations in the production of knowledge and innovation, and meeting the basic needs of the poor, especially in developing countries.

It is clear that this outlined theory of inclusive innovation is predominantly political because it focuses on the social relations of the production and distribution of new knowledge, innovative goods and services. It therefore presents inclusion not simply as an abstract ideal but a concrete and relational condition framed in non-ideal terms of justice. This is an approach that existing theories of justice (including libertarianism, liberal egalitarianism, utilitarianism and the capability approach) cannot grasp. Critical review of their arguments, and an interrogation of the assumptions behind these, reveals a lack of socio-political foundations and an unsustained idealism. Liberal egalitarians, libertarians, utilitarians and some capability theorists remain constructivists and are therefore unable to theorise a non-ideal system of social relations in innovation. In this sense, they can be of no help when it comes to offering a new normative framework of transformative change for national systems of innovation. As a result, such systems remain hierarchical and top down, failing to recognise and take into account the needs and interests of the poor and/or disadvantaged populations.

A smarter 'needs-based' approach to inclusive innovation would not only be able to meet the justice requirement of taking the situation and interests of everyone into account, it would also able to do so by following non-ideal principles of equity, recognition and participation. A 'basic needs' approach requires that innovation cease to be driven by effective demand for luxurious technological goods and services which can increase profits within capitalism for a tiny minority of people at the expense of the social equality, cohesion and environmental sustainability of the vast majority. Instead, innovation can concentrate on meeting the basic needs of the majority of people in society who are not necessarily interested in luxuries but in practical and equitable solutions to their everyday problems in a number of sectors, including those of health, food, energy and transport. Emerging models of innovation in developing countries such as India and Brazil constitute alternatives to the top-down hierarchical innovations of developed countries, which focus on the aspirations and needs of the richest 1% of the global population. In this sense, emerging models of innovation are models from below which can have a transformative impact on equalising social relations at the BoP. Whether they be frugal innovations, grassroots innovations or, indeed, more institutional social innovations, emerging models of innovation have one common element: they all challenge established hierarchies and global value chains. In this sense, they enable justice in the developing world. However, the need for a plausible framework of evaluation remains. Not every emerging innovation can be taken to be inclusive by definition. From this it also follows that not every emerging innovation should be supported by public policy.

The set of non-ideal principles of justice in innovation proposed in this book can help efforts towards the effective evaluation of institutional frameworks and processes. Although equity, recognition and participation in themselves cannot lead directly to a perfectly just innovation process, they can guide society towards identifying current injustices in innovation (such as the health needs of poor people neglected by the system) and improving social relations in national systems of innovation (such as equalising relations between innovators and publics). Public action and campaigning for inclusive innovation constitute the very sources of non-ideal principles of equity, participation and recognition. As such they involve struggles for equal access to both the production and consumption of innovations which meet basic human needs. The empirical cases of public action and campaigning for both high- and low-tech innovation analysed in this book are crucial for the promotion of critical thinking around established top-down ideals. I have argued that the latter ought to be replaced by bottom-up frameworks within which people are recognised as rights-bearing social actors who participate in equal relations of innovation. Politics and the state should embed this bottom-up framework into institutions that help people to meet their basic needs through innovation. Although many traditional innovation studies refer to the state, they do so only in passing and we therefore need to follow those scholars who recognise the importance of state structures for inclusive innovation.

Certainly, developing an effective evaluative framework of inclusive innovation based on equity, recognition and participation will not be an easy task. First, there is a need to replace traditional manuals such as the Frascati and Patent Manuals with (new quantitative and qualitative) indicators and measures. Second, these new indicators have to be able to move beyond resources, and towards measuring the level of equality in social relations in innovation. Third, the informational basis for assessments of inclusive innovation needs to be clarified. Fourth, all these new indicators must then be tested in practice.

An effective evaluative framework of inclusive innovation should take on board key methodological principles of innovation benchmarking, including focus, differentiation, measurement and learning. Any practical exercise should, of necessity, be concerned with the input/output/impact of inclusive innovation. Unless inclusive innovation models are redistributive, they will fail to equalise social relations in innovation. While it is certainly true that justice never pays in one currency, it is also true that it is social relations that matter most in innovation systems.

Index

114   *Index*